-8 99

how to be a
better....

negotiator

THE INDUSTRIAL SOCIETY

The Industrial Society stands for changing people's lives. In nearly eighty years of business, the Society has a unique record of transforming organisations by unlocking the potential of their people, bringing unswerving commitment to best practice and tempered by a mission to listen and learn from experience.

The Industrial Society's clear vision of ethics, excellence and learning at work has never been more important. Over 10,000 organisations, including most of the companies that are household names, benefit from corporate Society membership.

The Society works with these, and non-member organisations, in a variety of ways – consultancy, management and skills training, in-house and public courses, information services and multi-media publishing. All this with the single vision – to unlock the potential of people and organisations by promoting ethical standards, excellence and learning at work.

If you would like to know more about the Industrial Society please contact us.

The Industrial Society
48 Bryanston Square
London
W1H 7LN
Telephone 0171 262 2401

The Industrial Society is a Registered Charity No. 290003

how to be a
better....
negotiator

John Mattock & Jöns Ehrenborg

Illustrations: Ingrid Hoffsten

First published in 1996
Reprinted 1997, 1998

Kogan Page Limited
120 Pentonville Road
London N1 9JN

© John Mattock and Jons Ehrenborg, 1996

British Library Cataloguing in Publication Data
A CIP record for this book is available from the British Library
ISBN 0 7494 2093 6

Typeset by Photoprint, Torquay, Devon
Printed in England by Clays Ltd, St Ives plc

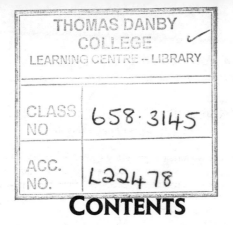
CONTENTS

HOW TO BE A BETTER ... SERIES

Whether you are in a management position or aspiring to one, you are no doubt aware of the increasing need for self-improvement across a wide range of skills.

In recognition of this and sharing their commitment to management development at all levels, Kogan Page and the Industrial Society have joined forces to publish the How to be a Better ... series.

Designed specifically with your needs in mind, the series covers all the core skills you need to make your mark as a high-performing and effective manager.

Enhanced by mini case studies and step-by-step guidance, the books in the series are written by acknowledged experts who impart their advice in a practical way which encourages effective action.

Now you can bring your management skills up to scratch *and* give your career prospects a boost with the How to be a Better ... series!

Titles available are:

How to be Better at Giving Presentations
How to be a Better Problem Solver
How to be a Better Interviewer
How to be a Better Teambuilder
How to be Better at Motivating People
How to be a Better Decision Maker
How to be a Better Communicator
How to be a Better Negotiator

Forthcoming titles are:

How to be a Better Project Manager
How to be a Better Creative Thinker

Available from all good booksellers. For further information on the series, please contact:

Kogan Page, 120 Pentonville Road, London N1 9JN
Tel: 0171 278 0433   Fax: 0171 837 6348

INTRODUCTION

HOW TO USE THIS BOOK

There are course books that teach you car maintenance as you sit in your armchair, helping you become a theoretical expert without ever getting your hands grimy. There are also fault-finding manuals – how to diagnose the symptoms of over-heating or the loss of power in third gear and what to do about them. And there are hobby books and magazines full of fascinating facts about the development of the V8 engine or the racing advantages of a hardened suspension.

This book is a bit of all three: you can read it from front to back and improve yourself as a negotiator; you can refer to it for specific ideas on how to solve topical problems during your next negotiation; or you can pass a pleasant half hour browsing and perhaps pick up a useful tip or two.

For those who want to read the text from front to back, we have organised the material in a sequence. We focus first on *the players*, then move on to *the game, getting ready*, and *at the table*. The very first section is about *yourself*, in the spirit of the inscription above the door of the Oracle at Delphi: *gnôthi seautón* (know thyself).

If you want to use the book as a fault-finding tool, the contents page will guide you to the chapter you need. The weaknesses and worries expressed in the 16 key statements ('I worry about not getting the best deal possible', for example) have come from observing thousands of participants on communications train-ing courses: when we are teaching managers how to be better negotiators, these are the issues that trouble them.

Perhaps you like to dip and dabble. Nothing wrong with that. This book is unusual in that you can start reading practically anywhere and it still makes sense. There are frequent cross-references between sections, marked >> *Creative bargaining*, page 67, for example. The reference is not usually to a whole chapter, but rather to one of the ideas developed within the section – usually highlighted, or in a *What this means to you* panel. You might enjoy wandering back and forth through the network of interlocking themes.

The examples and case studies we offer are drawn from history, current affairs, family life, literature and, of course, business. Please think about the examples and try to convert them to match your own experience and expectations: if you are working on labour negotiations within a factory in Stevenage, you might have something to learn from how people negotiate the sale of mobile telephone networks in China.

THE PERSON ACROSS THE TABLE

We have had to decide what to call the person you are negotiating with. 'Enemy' is clearly wrong. 'Partner' has been fashionable for some years, but we find it pious. 'Counterpart' becomes clumsy in use, and we can't just talk about 'them' all the time.

We try throughout to encourage a win:win approach, and stress the need to work at developing empathy with the person across the table. Realistically, we accept that this person might want to play tough or even fight dirty.

So we have chosen the word 'opponent'. Your opponent is positioned across from you when the negotiation begins; it is your job as a creative negotiator to step around to his side. Then perhaps he *will* be your partner.

THE DEAL YOU ARE LOOKING FOR — WHAT WE MEAN BY WIN:WIN

This is very simple. You come away from a good negotiation with major gains and minor losses. So does your opponent.

How is this possible? Because of the *differences* between you: different needs, different perceptions, different resources, different pressures.

Because of these differences, you and your opponent attach different values to different items. During your preparations and discussions, you come to understand these variations.

Then you trade off: you yield on matters which are painless for you to concede, but which matter greatly to your opponent, while he offers you goodies which mean a lot you but cost him little to provide. Win:win.

But there are dangers and difficulties along the way. Good luck!

1

YOURSELF

'I'm not comfortable as a negotiator; it isn't me'

In our experience, this means one of two things. Either you are a pushy, impatient person, who is bad at listening and bad at sharing, or – far more likely – you see yourself as weak, diffident and a natural victim.

On management training courses, working with case studies and real-life examples, we see many people who are poor negotiators for the first reason. They kill potential deals through greed and intransigence, they damage working relationships with their arrogance, and they perpetuate the myth that negotiation is combat. Often, such people think they're getting it right, and that all they need to pick up from the advanced negotiations seminar is a few handy little dirty tricks. They never say 'Negotiating isn't my scene.' Instead they say: 'I'm so strong and clever that my opponent can't keep up with my strategies.' With these students we work a lot on *sensitivity*.

At the opposite pole, there are those who see negotiation as a dangerous black art, practised by people who are somehow braver and more knowledgeable. With these students we work on *assertiveness*.

You undoubtedly have your own bundle of attitudes and even hang-ups, and we cannot treat them from between the pages of a book. Instead, we offer advice on how you can make sure that your discomfort ('negotiating isn't me') doesn't damage the negotiating process – and your outcome – too much.

Here we address both extremes on our spectrum: the overconfident and the diffident.

ADVICE TO THE OVERCONFIDENT

The whole world of business, and particularly the cultures of the big corporations, set great store by confidence. Confident people are admired – they are the dynamic protagonists who feature in the business magazines. In the companies which these superstars control, confident people get promoted: 'We like guys who lead from the front.' Many managers these days suffer from serious overconfidence.

Great confidence in yourself is invaluable when you are selling, politicking or exercising leadership. When you are negotiating, just a little bit too much confidence can have you shooting yourself in the foot.

The most likely mistake for you to make in a negotiation is this: when you are setting your targets you set them too high, and forget to plan ways to climb down. You think, 'Well, we're going to get what we want anyway, so what's the point of talking about concessions?' So before you start the negotiation, you've painted yourself into a corner. Then when the talking begins, you confidently open the bargaining with a demand that sounds, not to put too fine a point on it, greedy. And you don't put too fine a point on it – that's not your confident way. You just slap it on the table – 'Here – this is what we want!' (You have already made some pretty confident guesses about what your opponent wants from the deal – in fact you probably know better than he does what's good for him.) When your opponent suggests that you might moderate your requirements, you respond with 'Climb down? Me? You don't mess me around like that!' So you can't move, so you don't reach agreement (>> *Movement*, page 130).

Perhaps we exaggerate slightly, but if you recognise yourself at all in that description, you must do something about it, to avoid getting locked in a vicious spiral.

Compensating for overconfidence: Tip 1

Make plans for a dignified climbdown – a face-saving formula.

If you aim high and your opponent aims high, you will both have to lower your sights at some point during the negotiation. When the time comes for you to make your concession, you will need a credible explanation.

Let's say you're selling electronic components, and you've opened the bidding at £18.50 per unit – pretty confident (!) that you'll settle somewhere around the £18 mark, which would give you a profit margin of £5.

It becomes clear during the negotiation that the customer doesn't need the goods as desperately as you thought he did, and he asks you to drop your price to £15.50 – otherwise he just won't buy any electronic components today. How can you justify a sudden drop of £3?

If you simply say 'OK, then – £15.50 it is', the implication is clear – 'When I asked for £18.50, I was just being greedy because I thought I had you over a barrel.' With that idea in the air, the deal is done in an atmosphere of grudges and suspicion.

So equip yourself in advance with a reason or pretext or excuse for your sudden change of heart: 'I can trim £3 off the price by eliminating the packaging costs'; 'I know one of our subsidiaries has an overstock position on this product – maybe I can channel some of them your way at a substantial discount'; 'If you can take delivery at a time to suit us, then we can optimise on production costs – maybe even getting the price down to the level you're asking.'

ADVICE TO THE DIFFIDENT

You have been negotiating all your life, with parents, siblings and friends – but if your image of yourself is shy, timid or submissive, you probably haven't enjoyed the negotiations.

Nothing we can say here will change a retiring person into a death-or-glory negotiator. We give advice elsewhere on how to become more assertive (>> *Talking and listening*, page 145).

Here we limit our advice to:

Compensating for diffidence: Tip 2

Get an assertive partner to coach you, and learn as you go along.

Professional writers are often rather other-worldly people, introverted and 'not very clever with money'. This is where literary agents come in. For the traditional 10 per cent, these good people negotiate with publishers on behalf of authors –

and they negotiate very hard, which tends to upset the publishers. Their style with their clients tends to be: 'You just keep on writing the lovely books, dear. Leave the dirty business to me.'

If you employ an agent as your negotiator, you will never learn. There is a compromise solution.

If you are about to enter a negotiation which you are uncomfortable with, find a 'good negotiator' – colleague or friend – to talk it through with. Choose somebody assertive but not aggressive, who will understand your difficulties. As an agenda for your conversation, see the chapters on *Planning* (page 73) and *Targets*, (page 91).

Then, stage by stage as the negotiation progresses, go back to your coach for consultation, encouragement and reassurance. Aim for a realistic, satisfying outcome from the bargaining phase (> > *Timetabling*, page 110).

This way of working will not only protect your interests in the negotiation itself, it will increase your confidence overall.

2

EMOTION

'I'm uncomfortable with conflict'

If you have done everything you can (> > *Handling the process*, page 113) to set an open atmosphere, and if you have signalled clearly your intention to play the win:win game in your negotiation, you have every chance of avoiding conflict. Every chance, but no guarantee. In any negotiation, you might have to face an opponent who seems to be comfortable with conflict. He:

❏ Ridicules your sincere offerings.
❏ Insists on *getting* before even thinking about *giving*.
❏ Sneers, sighs, snarls and slaps the table.
❏ Goes back on agreements you've made earlier.
❏ Blames you personally for shortcomings in your proposal.

All this nasty behaviour tends to come out during the bargaining phase. In fact, the opponent who resorts to this sort of misconduct usually tries to get straight into the nitty-gritty bargaining without much initial exploration and discussion. He prefers simple combat to the touchy-feely approach which we advocate, perhaps because it is more challenging to his intellect and emotions.

To respond intelligently it is essential to keep your cool – and the first step in doing that is to step back from the situation.

Conflict handling: Pointer 1 (why this behaviour?)

Retreat to a calm space and try to figure it out. Ask yourself (or your team-mates) 'Why is he behaving this way?'

The answer to that question will often be one of the following – or more likely a combination of elements from two or three.

He's playing win:lose. He wants to maximise gains for his side, and doesn't give a hoot for your welfare. All your win:win ideas sound to him like idealistic flim-flam – *if* he's even listened. Perhaps he has seen too many Wall Street/Cold War movies (> > *Ritual*, page 43).

There is a power imbalance. He is purchasing manager for Gargantua Inc. and you represent Negligible Enterprises. Or you are trying to sell him your house in a buyer's market. Or he has the monopoly on something you really need badly.

He just wants a quick fix. Your approach is perhaps based on an assumption that he doesn't share: that there are benefits to be got from a long-term relationship. He just wants to grab all he can and then it's goodbye for ever.

There's a monkey on his back. Aggressive behaviour is frequently an expression of fear. Perhaps his boss is a monster; perhaps he has a law suit hanging over him; perhaps he has sunk his last dollar in the project and feels he has no room left for manoeuvre in his negotiation with you.

He lacks respect for you. It might be you personally, or the reputation that has preceded you, or your age, sex, race or profession (alas!). Or perhaps he feels that your status fails to match his – that he is negotiating with an inferior.

He's a rude person. Perhaps he comes from a working culture that rewards aggressive attitudes; perhaps there is a lot of insecurity in his personal make-up, and he is using rudeness/ bluntness/aggression unconsciously as a shield. Or perhaps nobody ever taught him to say 'Please' and 'Thank you'.

These can all be distilled down to three possibilities: he sees the issues and goals differently from you; he has a different view of the negotiating process; or he doesn't have the same idea about good manners.

So during your time-out, decide what level of difficulty you are facing, and when you meet your opponent for the next round, act accordingly – and be prepared to show some steel.

Conflict handling: Pointer 2 (issues and goals)

Separate the problem problem from the people problem, and invite your opponent to discuss the problem problem.

'I understand how important it is to you to get the best possible deal, and I can see that the issue of guarantees/copyright/ overtime payments might be an obstacle. So perhaps we should try to find a fresh angle on that before we go any further. Tell me again how you see the issue . . .'

If you discover now that his goals really do not match yours, then don't bash your brains out against a brick wall. Either withdraw from the negotiation or adjust your goals and tactics – perhaps settling for simple bazaar-style haggling: if he opens at 20, and you open at 30, then 26 represents a good deal for you in the circumstances.

Conflict handling: Pointer 3 (the negotiating process)

Look for ways to move the business forward; invite him to help you.

'We seem to have hit a sticky patch here. Maybe if we rescheduled some of the agenda/asked Paco to join us/went back to our opening proposals, we could find a way to carry on . . . (>> *Handling the process*, page 113).

Conflict handling: Pointer 4 (manners)

Let him know that you are uncomfortable, that this might damage the outcome, and that he can do something about it.

Say:

> 'I have trouble working in this sort of atmosphere, and I really think we'll make better progress if we can avoid unnecessary friction. Can you see a way of moving on without unpleasantness? After a short break, perhaps?'

In every case, your tone should be calm but assertive, you should be offering a positive way forward, and you should be involving your opponent in the solution to the impasse: 'I'm inviting you to help me solve this problem'.

You should have in the back of your mind the exit route you have planned, in case further bad behaviour makes a negotiated settlement impossible (> > *Planning: BATNA*, page 88).

Conflict handling: Pointer 5 (showing steel)

Let your opponent know that you are not prepared to be pushed around any longer.

At an early stage of the dealings, you should have made it implicitly clear that you intend to negotiate as an equal, that you are competent, and that you know what you want.

Unfortunately, a self-centred opponent might not notice your implicit signals. If he comes on too strong in the bargaining phase, you might have to show him your strength in a more direct way. This does not mean shouting back!

Say:

'I hope you realise that I can close this negotiation at any time.'

'If you can't meet our needs in any way, and if your organisation really does want to do business, I would be happy to meet somebody on your side who is able to act more flexibly.'

'In spite of what you seem to think, I do know what I'm talking about. If you can't accept that, then we really are wasting our time here. Perhaps you'd like to meet another representative of my company?'

'I am not afraid of bluster. If it makes you feel better to let off steam, go ahead.'

'Perhaps you're trying to tell me that we can't close this gap. I'm convinced we can, and I don't like walking away from a negotiation. I'll call you in a couple of days to see if we can fix another meeting.'

In all the examples above, we have cast you in the reactive role – your opponent firing *negative* emotions in your direction, leaving you to find ways of defusing the situation.

Let us now consider how you might yourself help bring about a positive result, by bringing *positive* emotions into play at every opportunity.

Emotional advice: 1

Use emotions positively; express them openly at chosen moments.

Many people are natural and enthusiastic communicators away from work – when they are discussing family matters, football or their latest love affair.

Fewer people are able to express natural enthusiasm at the office – a result of social conditioning which says: self-control is adult; adult is professional; professional is good.

An average communicator moves in childhood from untutored emotion and spontaneity – 'childish' or 'amateurish' behaviour – to a more repressed style which gains the approval of his teachers, workmates, neighbours. There he stops, and this is the style he brings into a negotiation with him: grown-up, non-creative and boring.

An excellent communicator goes one step further. He learns all the necessary lessons during his social-professional conditioning – don't rock the boat/don't frighten the horses/don't raise a stink – but refuses to have emotional capacity crushed out of him. He is ready and able to display raw feelings when it is useful to do so.

He knows how to:

❏ Express *delight* when things are going well: 'You know, I think it's really great how much progress we're making already.'
❏ Express *dismay* when misunderstandings occur: 'I hate to see a deal like this threatened by poor communication.'

❏ Show *anger* with third parties who are causing unnecessary difficulties: 'Your head office said *what*?!? Do they think you and I have been working on this deal for the last three weeks just so they can suffocate it with paperwork? Maybe we should take a break while I catch my breath.'

❏ Display *fervour* as the final agreement gets closer: 'I tell you, I'm really excited by the prospects for this deal.'

❏ *Commiserate* with an opponent during setbacks: 'I sympathise with your predicament, and I'd love to help you find a way out.'

❏ *Celebrate* at the personal level when a good agreement has been reached: 'This means a lot to me, and I'm happy for both of us.'

Emotions can break a deadlock where purely mental efforts have failed. Here is an apocryphal story to make the point:

During the design and construction of the Anglo-French supersonic airliner, there were many negotiating committees in action, including one general purposes committee to deal with all the bits and pieces. To them fell the seemingly simple decision of the spelling – 'Concord', as in the English word, or 'Concorde' as the French have it.

On one side of the table, first class minds developed at Eton and Balliol College; on the other, superbly trained graduates of the École Nationale d'Administration. They approached the issue from every angle and tried every intellectual technique they could muster in an attempt to debate the matter constructively. But effectively there was nothing to say: obviously the British were mandated to go for the English spelling; of course the French wanted their beautiful language displayed on the beautiful aeroplane.

Finally one of the French delegates became so frustrated at the stupidity of it all that a tear rolled down his cheek. Immediately all

continued overleaf

continued from previous page

three Englishmen leapt to their feet in paroxysms of embarrassment: 'But monsieur, if it means so much to you, of course you must have your E on the end ... but please stop crying ...'

And a first-hand story of negotiating with the Chinese, told to us by a seasoned, white-haired campaigner:

The day had been going remarkably well: seven items on the agenda, and our side had come out well over expectations on most of them. I felt I was on a winning streak, and suggested that we now discuss an eighth, unscheduled item.

Outrage from the Chinese side: all agenda items had to be cleared at least two weeks in advance.

I offered apologies for the disruption, and then said 'But you see, I had always intended to include this item on today's agenda, but I am an old man, and old men sometimes forget.' They gave me what I wanted.

Emotional advice: 2

Make allowances for your own irrationality.

The opposite of 'emotion' is 'logic' or 'reason'. As has been noted above, we are conditioned in our professional lives to respect reason, justify our decisions on grounds of logic, and pretend that emotion has nothing to do with it.

But a negotiation is not an either–or situation. The rational and emotional are intertwined.

A rational approach will set the targets for a negotiation, and measure its outcome, in purely material or financial terms. Yet there is a value within the negotiation process itself – an apparently irrational value – which can affect the process and the result.

This is sometimes called *transactional value*: a sense of having got a fair deal can be more important than rational self-interest. Try this exercise:

1. A shopkeeper offers you a pack of video cassettes for £10. You know there is a store a few minutes' drive away where you can get exactly the same for £7 – 30 per cent less. Would you make the journey?
2. A shopkeeper offers you a video-recorder for £1,000. You know there is a store a few minutes' drive away where you can get exactly the same for £997 – 0.3 per cent less. Would you make the journey?

Most people say yes to Question 1 and no to Question 2.

In the first case, the motivation to go to the other store is not a purely rational desire to save £3. A £3 saving is available in the second case, too – rationally the same reward for the same few minutes in your car. The real motivation is something like: 'I won't enjoy using these video tapes if I feel I've been suckered.'

In the second case, you are in the store, face to face with the salesman, and about to spend big money on a luxury item. Most people are disinclined to spoil the experience by acting like a cheapskate.

It is often difficult to convince people that they act irrationally in negotiations. Participants on training courses usually insist to the bitter end that all their moves are considered, wise and purposeful. They would drive around the block to save 30 per cent, but not to save 0.3 per cent, they say – a rational distinction. But you don't carry percentages in your pocket, you carry money, and for £3, however you save it, you can buy a cup of coffee and a piece of cheesecake.

WHY TAKEOVERS HAPPEN

In the 1980s, there was a spate of aggressive acquisitions internationally by British companies, particularly in the North American market.

While American nationalists fumed at the Limey invasion of Fortress America, a London business school made a study of dozens of such operations. They asked the question: what made the takeover – an expensive and exhausting exercise in negotiation – worth all the trouble?

To acquire technical know-how; to make the acquiring company look dynamic and boost its share value; to increase market share: all these were mentioned. But the business school's report concluded that, in most cases, the real reason for the takeover was to *feed the emotional needs of the President and/or the CEO.*

WHAT THIS MEANS TO YOU

Recognise the irrational demon inside yourself: nothing you do is 100 per cent logical.

Take that irrationality into account during your planning, and accept that your emotions will affect your judgement, and probably transmit themselves to your opponent across the table.

Remember, your opponent is reacting to you not only at the conscious level – listening to the things you say and thinking about them coolly – he is also tuned in to the sub-verbal signals you are sending out.

So a vicious circle can easily start: you *think* you have explained your position rationally, but your uncontrolled emotions add a certain flavour to what you have said; he *feels* your emotions, and reacts to them in what he thinks is a rational way, but his emotions and the echo of your original emotions distort the message; you *feel* these distortions, and react.

This why the key manoeuvre at any moment of emotional stress is to call a time-out. Get some distance. Find space. Have a cooling-off period. Break the vicious circle.

Emotional advice: 3

Instincts, impulses and intuition are there to help you.

How often it happens in life and in the movies: 'Get on to old Harry, and ask him what his gut feeling is on this.'

Old Harry doesn't just have his guts to go by. Sometimes he *feels* his blood run cold. He has been known to *smell* a rat. He always has his *ear* to the ground, and he never fails to *see* the writing on the wall. In his heyday as a negotiator, Harry was never afraid to play a hunch, and they often turned out right – the ones that didn't left a nasty *taste* in his mouth. There are those who say Harry has a highly developed *sixth sense*, and maybe he has . . .

WHAT THIS MEANS TO YOU

Pay heed to your instincts during your negotiation. If you feel a rush of optimism, that might be a good time to suggest a raising of the stakes; if your positive proposals sound hollow when you voice them, then it might be time to start exploring compromise options.

Please note: to act on impulse is not the same as acting impulsively. If you feel an impulse, you should take time to think it over. But don't crush it or discard it: it could lead you to exactly the breakthrough you are looking for.

3

PEOPLE

'I don't know how to handle this opponent'

This whole book has a people thread running through it. In this section we limit ourselves to the idea of *reaching your opponent*. This idea is much more than just manipulation; you will make much greater progress as a negotiator if you genuinely like people and want the best for them.

The old psychology professor said: 'When young people come and ask me if I'll accept them for a degree course, I ask them why they want to study psychology. The great majority say it's because they're interested in people. I say: "Sorry, in my faculty we study statistics and rats. If it's people you're interested in, English Literature is along the street and left at the traffic lights." '

His point was clear: people are very complicated, and if you want to study their behaviour from the printed page or in the lecture hall, your best bet is the play, the short story, or the novel. (And not just English literature: Ibsen? O. Henry? Vikram Seth? Try one as an alternative to the next Business Guru Blockbuster).

Rats and statistics go together quite well. People are a different story. Do you like it if somebody claims to have you taped, and know exactly what you're going to say and do next? Nobody does.

ANIMAL BEHAVIOUR

Certain reactions are built into all of us:

❏   If another member of the species is aggressive towards us, we either get aggressive back or run away.
❏   We can't take an interest in sophisticated inducements until our basic needs are catered for – try throwing a stick for a frightened dog or dangling a fluffy ball of wool in front of a hungry cat! – but once we feel safe and well fed, we are inquisitive, and ready for a bit of fun.

❏ We are a tribal animal, rather than solitary, and respond to social imperatives.
❏ The males of the species like to show off.

Ethologists are scientists who study animal behaviour. They might make good negotiators, especially if they specialise in the higher primates. Desmond Morris's book *The Naked Ape*, was a bestseller among business people all over the world.

WHAT THIS MEANS TO YOU

Don't be fooled by the business suit and briefcase: the negotiating opponent you are about to face is an animal.

Don't be aggressive, because then he'll have to fight or run away.

Make sure he is comfortable before you start the clever business.

Respect his territory: no messy demonstrations of vacuum pumps on his nice clean desk (or multi-media presentations from your laptop?).

Admire his prowess and make it clear that you do.

HUMAN BEHAVIOUR: COMMUNICATION TYPES

As for psychologists, many have tried to find patterns in human behaviour and produce predictive models. How useful it would be to know exactly what the other guy is going to do next!

The psychologists have had varying degrees of success. One of the most durable attempts is the Myers–Briggs type indicator, which uses four polarities to categorise 16 personality types. The

MBTI suits the world of negotiation very well, if we focus on two of the polarities: *Sensor–Intuitor,* and *Thinker–Feeler.*

When we are interested in reaching our opponent, we must ask: 'What sort of argument might influence him?'

Reaching your opponent: Step 1

Resist the temptation to pretend he is just like you.

The world would be a much kinder and safer and easier place if everybody had the same perceptions and drives as me! To reduce anxiety, we often pretend that this is the case – carrying a cosy cocoon of self-deception around with us.

The danger in communication is clear: if you are the sort of person who responds to cool, logical, short-term arguments (a *sensor/thinker*), you will be tempted to use the same style when you are trying to persuade others.

But surely, if you are faced with a dreamy, inspirational *intuitor/feeler*, you run the risk of actually turning him off.

Reaching your opponent: Step 2

Work out which of the four types he is.

Pick up evidence early: the way he answers the phone and lays out his faxes; his tone of voice and presence or absence of humour; what his office looks like and how his colleagues address him; how he wants the agenda organised, and which of your statements and suggestions get him sitting up and taking notice.

Plot him along these two axes: which quadrant does he fall in?

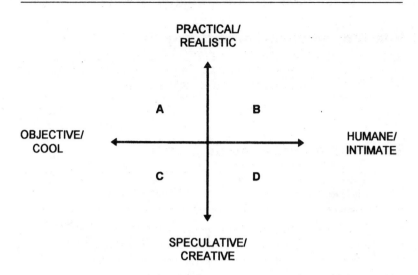

Different professions attract different types.

❏ Many university teachers are Cs;
❏ Many nurses are the B type.
❏ Type A doesn't produce very good advertising copy-
    writers;
❏ If your financial controller is a type D, you could be in
    trouble.

A word of warning here from Gordon Lawrence, a specialist in
MBTI:

> As soon as we learn type concepts, we see the value of estimating
> people's types so as to reach them better ... treat your guess as a
> hypothesis to be checked out, then listen carefully and be ready to
> change your guess.

This is very similar to the model-building strategy we offer in
Culture, page 51. A good negotiator takes his opponent's culture
and personality into account, but constantly revises his esti-
mates.

Reaching your opponent: Step 3

Organise your arguments to suit his type.

A	B
Adopt an impersonal tone Tackle 'how'/'what' questions Talk of real benefits now Expect critical questions Don't bluff	Use a warm, friendly tone Talk of lasting relationship Emphasise harmony and agreement Cite successes elsewhere Offer to go the extra mile
C	**D**
Focus on *his* big picture Invite the exploration of options Stress long-term benefits Expect to be probed in depth Don't presume	Build sincerity and warmth Match his posture and tone Play *his* vision back to *him* Focus on people possibilities Tailor the details to suit *him*

4

RELATIONSHIPS

'It's difficult working with people I don't know'

First: don't think you're the only one who feels this way.

Some people are more extrovert than others – which doesn't necessarily mean telling lots of loud jokes at parties. In personality theory, extroversion means 'deriving gratification from the physical and social environment'; an extrovert prefers sorting things out in contact with other people, while an introvert might be more inclined to analyse problems alone, drawing on his own resources. Nobody is a success in life without having a bit of both in his make-up, but it must be said that our working culture tends to reward and encourage extrovert behaviour, and this is particularly true in a negotiation.

There is a very good statistical chance that your opponent across the negotiating table is predominantly an introvert, battling to 'prove himself' by seeming bluff, outgoing, and totally in control of the situation.

If you are an introvert yourself, dealing with a genuine or quasi–extrovert, you should not try to compete in the same terms. Rather, you are in an ideal position to ask questions and listen attentively to the answers – one of the most difficult social and professional skills.

Building working relationships: Suggestion 1

Establish empathy, but don't get dragged into sympathy.

Your goal is to open up honest, clear and comfortable communication, in an atmosphere of mutual respect. This does not mean you have to agree with everything your opponent does, wants or claims. Consider an advocate defending a murderer, or a bank manager considering a small loan application from one of his customers.

Building working relationships: Suggestion 2

Ask genuine questions, and listen with interest to the answers.

In *The New International Manager* (Kogan Page, 1991 – Canning International Management Development), four layers of research are identified:

1. The background *culture* your opponent grew up in, and/or in which he now works.
2. The *commercial context* in which his business operates – the market, the legal and financial systems, the infrastructure.
3. His *company* and everything about it; what lies behind the CEO's statement in the last annual report?
4. His *character* and how that fits with the work he does: what is his definition of 'success'?; does he live and breathe his profession, or is it 'just a job'; is he a steady, analytical type, or does he operate largely on intuition? (>>*People*, page 34).

It is tricky to ask direct questions about 4; you just have to piece the picture together from observation. In connection with 1–3, however, it is quite professional to probe – all in the name of doing better business together.

Of course, you must be prepared to pay back in kind. If your opponent talks willingly and openly about his situation, you have to answer his questions about yours.

Building working relationships: Suggestion 3

Adjust your pacing to suit the local culture.

In some cultures, people spend a long time doing efficient business together before they begin to express friendship –

north-west Europe, for example. A 58-year-old native of Frankfurt would quite likely be embarrassed if you got your baby photographs out in the first coffee-break.

In other parts of the world – notably the Mediterranean – you might find your host inviting you out for dinner, and discussing life, death and the human condition before the negotiation even starts.

Try to match the local behaviour, while remaining true to yourself. (>>*Culture*, page 49).

Building working relationships: Suggestion 4

Give a little extra for the person, not just for the deal.

This does not mean producing empty cosmetic statements like 'I wouldn't do this for just anybody, Giuseppe, but since it's you and I like you I'm gonna make you an offer that'll blow your socks off.' They just annoy people. Nor does it mean dropping your price out of pity. You're negotiating as an equal here. But you *can* say:

> I always like to get personal satisfaction out of a piece of business, and I sense that you feel the same. And if we make a good agreement today, we'll probably be working together again before too long. So let's see if we can find a way to get round this budget problem of yours . . .

Building working relationships: Suggestion 5

Remember the little things.

If he tells you in February that he has a stressful presentation to make in March, ask him in April how it went. Remember a fiftieth birthday, a daughter's wedding, the birth of a grandchild.

Building working relationships: Suggestion 6

Respect his professional boundaries.

You go out for dinner together, get a little friendly, and discuss your children's education, the refugee problem, and your grandfather's bunions.

Next day in his office there is only cool efficiency.

That's OK; it's not a slap in the face. He just wants a clear space to manoeuvre in during the negotiation – freedom to be professionally demanding.

This is particularly likely to happen if there are colleagues present.

You should give him a pleasant smile and some good eye contact, and then revert to a more formal social register too. The progress you have made on the personal front will almost certainly help your communications, but not if you keep reminding him of it.

Building working relationships: Suggestion 7

Don't undermine his self-esteem; don't crow about your own cleverness.

Most particularly, when the negotiation is over and the deal is done, *never* say 'You know, I was prepared to yield a little more than I did . . .' He can only interpret this as 'You're not as clever as me and you're out of pocket as a result.'

It is no basis for a friendship.

Building working relationships: Suggestion 8

What you do is more important than what you say.

You can be charm itself at the negotiating table, but if you can't deliver on your promises your working relationship won't get off the ground.

5

RITUAL

'I don't know the rules of the game'

> Game Theory: The formalised study of rational action in situations where the welfare of each agent in a group depends on how other group members act. A game is specified by, for each participating agent, a set of permitted strategies and a set of preferences between outcomes. Agents are 'perfectly rational': in particular, they act so as to maximise expected utility ... each agent acts assuming that the other agents are rational and that they will act on the same assumption.

> *The Oxford Companion to Philosophy*

By this academic definition, negotiating is certainly a game. In a negotiating situation:

❑ Your 'welfare' depends on how your opponent acts, and his welfare depends on you.
❑ There is a set of 'permitted strategies' for you and for your opponent, and each of you has a 'set of preferences between outcomes' – meaning you both want a good deal ('utility') rather than a bad one.
❑ You are 'rational' in that you make your moves in the hopes of improving your outcome (but >> *Emotion*, page 26, where we examine the *irrational* element in negotiation).
❑ You have to assume that your opponent is rational, too. (A good chess player needs somebody at his own level to play with; his thinking is knocked off course when a novice opponent makes an inexplicable move.)

Please notice: the definition of Game Theory makes no mention of 'fun', or any satisfaction that might come from the game itself. We look at the idea of *transactional value* in another section (>> *Emotion*, page 27).

Whether the game is to be fun or not, you must learn the rules before you can play effectively. Once you know the rules, you can decide whether to observe the ritual in every detail, or suggest better ways of getting a result (>> *Handling the process*, page 113).

Learning the ritual: Lesson 1

Ask.

If you are negotiating with someone more experienced than you, take the initiative by asking him for guidance: 'What should be the next step, in your view?'

People are often afraid of 'exposing themselves' – appearing ignorant or weak – and use this as a reason not to ask such a question. 'My opponent will laugh at me/take advantage of me.' No, he won't.

If he is a 'fair play' negotiator, it is in his interests to make sure you are playing the same game as him, and at a similar level. He will find your candour refreshing, and suggest the best way to move the negotiation forward – and you will learn as you go along. (Westerners who have been negotiating deals in Russia and its former empire sometimes report that the negotiations were dragged out by their post-communist opponents – not as a strategy of attrition, but because they were using the process as a kind of business training course for themselves.)

If he is a 'hardball' negotiator, your candid question will disarm him; any dirty tricks he is considering will be hard to play if he is describing the process to you (> > *Truth* page 59).

There is one remaining possibility: he doesn't know any more about negotiating than you do. In that case, your question will be a magic moment: from now on we can work out our own way of dealing with the situation, and this is the beginning of a good working relationship.

Learning the ritual: Lesson 2

Find out if it's to be fair play or hardball.

We try to be realistic in this book – encouraging our readers to try for win:win negotiations whenever possible, but admitting that there are situations and people that won't play out this way.

Negotiation was developed by early man as a means of distributing territory, food and mates, they say – an alternative to wasteful warfare all the time. Since then, there have been local developments – differences in the ritual from market to market, industry to industry, region to region.

But beneath all the variations, there are two basic approaches – *competitive/distributive* (which we will call hardball) and *collaborative/creative* (which we will call fair play).

Hardball	**Fair play**
Tough/macho	Gentle/feminine
Distributive: analyse and divide	Creative: integrate and grow
Play zero-sum game	Enlarge the pie
$(4 - 2 - 2 = 0)$	$(2 + 2 = 5)$
Haggle over each item	Negotiate the whole package
State positions	Explore interests
Dominate	Share

In the early stages of the negotiation, or even from signals you receive before the real negotiating begins, you should pick up clues as to which game your opponent wants to play. Of course, he might 'smile, and smile, and be a villain'; on the other hand, he might be a highly generous person with a gruff manner. Otherwise, if he displays one piece of behaviour from either of the above columns, he is likely to display the others before long.

If your experienced opponent presents a typewritten agenda, and unsmilingly suggests that you work through it step by step without preliminary discussion, you can get ready for plenty of pushy tactics later.

Learning the ritual: Lesson 3

If in doubt, be more rather than less formal.

The word 'ritual' comes from 'rite' – a custom or practice of a formal kind.

The ritual of negotiation does imply some level of formality; if we say 'We should negotiate with them over this', it gives a more formal picture than when we say 'I'm gonna have this out with them', or 'Let's tell them they're too expensive, and see what they say'.

This formality can be useful – preventing us from losing our temper, saying things on the spur of the moment that we might regret later, upsetting our opponent unduly. If we are negotiating on behalf of other people – union members, for example – the formality of the negotiating ritual is a signal to these constituents: the rules are being observed; we are working hard on your behalf; this negotiation is no picnic, Brother.

As a rule, it is best to start quite formally, and try to relax the atmosphere step by step until you find a level at which you and your opponent are both comfortable. If you begin as Mr Truman and Ms Bowles, you can be Harry and Sally later, and it feels like progress. But it's difficult to go backwards.

Learning the ritual: Lesson 4

Value the ritual for its own sake.

Ritual is important to people. Ask any anthropologist.

In a given culture, the rituals of courtship and marriage are important social markers. They show us the boundaries to acceptable behaviour.

The ritual of a military parade is a message to allies and enemies: 'Look how strong and well organised we are.' It is a way of displaying power without spilling blood.

But courtship, weddings and the military parade offer intrinsic satisfaction, too; people enjoy them for their own sake.

The same is true in negotiation: if you observe Lessons 1 and 2 above, you will soon learn all you need to know about the boundaries to your behaviour in the negotiation – the do's and don'ts – and how the power is distributed between you and your opponent, like who's buying and who's selling.

But never forget that the ritual is also valued in itself. There is more pleasure in a successful mushroom hunt than in going to the supermarket and buying 300g of mushrooms.

6

CULTURE

'I'm on alien territory and that hampers me'

To be working in a foreign culture is of course disturbing. Everything takes longer, costs more effort, is more stressful, and gives dubious results. Try signing your name with the wrong hand. It feels like that a lot of the time.

'A foreign culture' does not always mean 'people who were born and brought up in a different country'. You are in a foreign culture if you are a salesman working with research engineers, a woman working among men, a representative of HQ working in a local subsidiary, or a manager from a small company working within a corporate monolith. (The advice here is simple: don't make assumptions; keep your wits about you; learn from your mistakes; when in doubt, admit your ignorance and use charm.)

However, in this section we do take culture to mean: the unwritten rules that shape the social environment in a given country or region. Yes, we're talking about foreigners.

When we grow up in the social environment of our home country, we are equipped with rules of conduct, and a set of lenses and filters through which to view the world.

Likewise our opponent. If we understand *his* rules and lenses and filters better, we are better equipped to understand what makes him tick – and so do a better job of negotiating with him.

Why does a Mexican tick differently from a Korean?

We all know the dangers of racism, and this understanding has grown in the last generation. The vogue for 'politically correct' language is partly a result of this trend: we must cleanse our systems of negative stereotypes and prejudices. But in doing so, we must not ignore cultural differences – differences in how people perceive things, and what they expect from other people.

During the 1970s many middle-aged European executives found themselves in new international jobs – which meant dusting off their schoolroom English so they could do the business. They went on English courses.

One of your authors was an English teacher at the time, working with managers like these, and he set out determined to eschew the stereotypes. He did not want to believe that

Germans are orderly and precise, or that the French go in for philosophical over-elaboration, or that Italians are hypochondriac travellers. Alas, he found that there is no smoke without fire.

Germans *are* more averse to chaos than, say, the Irish. The French *do* place more emphasis on academic logic than, say, the Norwegians. And if Italians are uncomfortable, they tend to tell you so, leaving the British with their stiff upper lips to put up with bad service, lousy coffee and a shameful railway system.

Prejudices are generally held to be damaging; stereotypes make us insensitive and inflexible. The right approach to another culture is to set about building a model.

Cultural insights: 1 (model building)

Build a model of a culture.

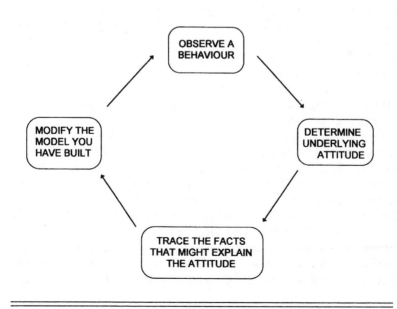

Facts: Population density; economic history; family/tribal structure; religion; topography; climate, etc.

Attitudes (and values): Business before pleasure? Or vice-versa?; Naturally rebellious? Or happy subordinates?; Punctual and orderly? Or lackadaisical and chaotic?

Behaviour: Do they stick to the agenda? Make jokes about the boss? Invite you home for dinner? Insist on having everything in writing?

You can buy 'cross-culture' books at the airport to tell you you mustn't touch a Thai's head, or show the soles of your feet to a Gulf Arab, or give a Russian an even number of flowers. You can learn these taboos as isolated examples of good manners.

It is much more fulfilling to ask the question 'Why?' and ferret around for some sort of answer.

Nobody really knows why the Japanese love to give and receive elaborately wrapped gifts, in which the packaging might be worth more than the contents. Perhaps it's because over-crowded Japan cut down all the trees to make farmland, and so paper is of great value and held in esteem as a material. And shortage of timber must also have meant shortage of fuel – perhaps explaining why so much Japanese cuisine uses energy-efficient cooking methods. As you build a model of Japanese attitudes and behaviour, how much might be explained from a starting point of land shortage and overcrowding (topographical/demographic data)? By the way, the Russians, who have plenty of space and lots of trees, traditionally don't bother to wrap a gift up. Build a different model for the Russians ...

There is no single explanation for why the Swedes are so given to consensus decision-making, rather than encouraging individuals to push decisions forward. Their Lutheran back-ground produces a heavy bias against ostentation and the arbitrary exercise of power: 'Stop showing off, Lars!' The industrial revolution came late, and when it came it was largely based on high-tech products – produced by an educated workforce who expected to be consulted about decisions that would affect them – the great-grandparents of today's middle managers. Any of these facts (religious, social, historical, economic) can provide a useful starting point for model building, and once you start to build your model, you can try clicking in new pieces of evidence: pea soup, pancakes and fruit preserves are a traditional Swedish meal on a Thursday; 'Welcome!' in Swedish English means 'We look forward to seeing you here in Sweden!'; in Sweden, if you want to buy a bottle of wine to go with your Sunday lunch, you have to buy it on Friday. And incidentally, don't the Japanese have a reputation for consensus decision making? It's a process called *Nemawashi*. Is that similar to the Swedish habit? Rebuild your model of the Japanese . . .

The whole exercise of cultural model building should be driven by curiosity; you have to want to know. In 1980 a curious traveller was motoring across White Russia (Belarus).

> Already the country . . . was slow, impersonal and absolute. I could not help wondering what effect such isolation might have on its inhabitants . . . Was the easy Russian submission to God or tyranny, I wondered, the result of a people crushed by the sheer size of their land? Could it be that the meandering, mystical, rough-hewn qualities of the Russian psyche – Russian novels, Russian music – that the unwieldy immensity of Russian bureaucracy . . .

> Colin Thubron, *Among the Russians*

Cultural insights: 2 (starting point)

Where to start your model.

The point of departure for all the gurus who write about 'cultural differences in business' is the writings of Edward and Mildred Hall in the late 1960s. The Halls studied the working cultures of most West European countries, and in *The Silent Language*, they divide them up according to two key concepts:

High context vs Low context
Polychronic vs Monochronic

High context communicators suppose that the people they are talking to are wise to the context in which the message is set: my listeners have a good idea what this is all about, and if they don't know they can guess. So in high context cultures ideas are not spelled out in detail. People piece together the whole message within the context they understand, and try not to bore each other with step-by-step explanations. Communication depends to a great extent on facial expressions, body language, inflexions of the voice, eye contact. Those raised in such an atmosphere can get impatient with low context communicators.

Low context communicators like to spell things out, and to have things spelt out to them. Sentences are completed. Only one person speaks at a time. Telephone agreements are confirmed by fax. These people sometimes think that high context communicators are chaotic, secretive, unreliable, emotional.

In *polychronic* cultures, people answer the phone, drink coffee, transmit sign language to their colleagues, listen to your presentation, and think about lunch all at once. They get bored and restless if only one thing is happening.

In *monochronic* cultures, timetables are respected and activities are carefully compartmentalised.

Hall examines France and Northern Germany, and finds the French to be high context/polychronic, and the Germans to be low context/monochronic.

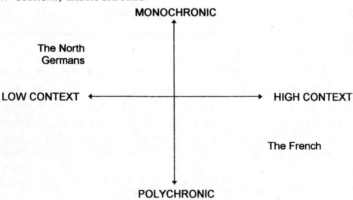

We find that when cultural friction occurs between people, it is usually a problem of communication or of timing: 'They're not making themselves clear ... what's going on? ... He's so stiff and correct, he can't possibly be creative ... If they're always late with their phone calls, what about their deliveries? ... He's not concentrating; he keeps changing the subject!'

When you start building your model of a culture which is new to you, ask around – talk to compatriots of yours who have worked in the target culture, and talk to natives of the culture who have travelled widely and so have a detached view of their origins. They will give you a lot of valuable information, but probably in an awful jumble.

So that you can begin putting shape on the material, show them the grid, and explain what the axes mean – and then ask them where they would place the culture in question. (We have done this, and found the Greeks to be high context/monochronic and the Russians to be low context/polychronic.)

Cultural insights: 3 (open enquiry)

Discuss the culture question openly.

Once trust is established, you are quite at liberty to discuss cultural differences with your opponent.

Be genuinely curious about why systems and people work the way they do. Be prepared to talk about your own background in return.

Cultural insights: 4 (adapting)

Consider modifying your own act.

In other sections, we offer suggestions about how you might shape your messages to suit particular individuals (> > *People*, page 34; *Talking and listening*, page 146).

If you are a Finnish engineer negotiating with a Moroccan salesman, you will have a smoother ride if you can relax a bit. If you are an Irishman doing business in Switzerland, you should try and be on time.

CODE OF PRACTICE FOR DEALINGS ACROSS CULTURES

We appreciate and enjoy cultural diversity
We accept that our own perceptions are coloured by our upbringing, within our native culture
We try to empathise with our partner's point of view, knowing that it will be influenced by his background
We do some homework to understand that background better
We are open-minded; we do not dump a national stereotype on an individual
Once trust is established with our opponent, we openly discuss how our differing cultures might be affecting the issue
We remain cool and detached, keeping emotion at arm's length
We remain true to ourselves, avoiding the temptation to 'go native' or mimic our partner's mannerisms
We begin with a formal, polite manner, and await signals of informality from our partner
Simple, clear, direct, honest and open: this is the best style for communication across cultures
We plan our communications to eliminate the negative and accentuate the positive

7

TRUTH

'I sometimes feel they're lying to me'

During the SALT arms reduction negotiations, one difficult issue was this: would the Americans be permitted to watch and make sure that the Soviets really were decommissioning their nuclear weapons? The Americans, with a relatively open society, were happy for Russians to check what they were doing, but the more secretive Russians were extremely touchy (a trait of their culture): did the Americans doubt their word?

Somebody clever on the American side in the negotiation found an old Russian proverb for Ronald Reagan to pronounce in the next round of meetings: 'Trust, but verify.'

At about the same time, research showed that more than 60 per cent of Americans thought Reagan was lying about arms shipments to Iran and the funding of the Contras.

In business as in politics, a realist must always be prepared to encounter dishonesty. If you feel that you are negotiating with a liar, there are two obvious possibilities:

1. You're right – he is lying to you.
2. You're imagining it.

Somewhere between the two there are several other explanations:

3. Something in your opponent's background gives him a framework of truth and falsehood which is different from yours (>> *Culture*, page 49).
4. There's a communication problem, and his well-intentioned messages are getting garbled (>> *Talking and listening*, page 141).
5. He's feeling bad about some aspect of the deal and can't bring himself to broach it, so he sounds evasive and looks shifty.

Let us reflect on these possibilities in that order, then look at a diagnostic routine to find out what's really going on. (In this chapter we offer few hints on what to do once you have found out, but cross-refer you to other sections where you should find the remedies.)

Sources of mistrust: 1

Your opponent is lying to you.

In the world of politics, opposing negotiators are often in a state of fundamental disagreement – perhaps ideological or religious, perhaps based on racial prejudice, perhaps as a result of some ancient wrong that cannot be forgotten. In such cases, one or both sides might decide that aggression and subterfuge are justified.

In business, there are those who like to 'play hardball': 'All is fair in love, war and negotiation,' they say, and treat you accordingly.

With such people, it is unusual to find a directly provable untruth. It would be a stupid opponent who told you a lie which you could easily detect by checking. This section ends with a step-by-step method for flushing out deception (page 61).

More commonly, an opponent who wants to play a bit of tricky hardball with you will use legitimisation ploys – little twists in the truth which are impossible for you to disprove, but which justify his greedy stance.

If you have a bad hunch about your opponent, and he is making heavy demands on you, watch out for legitimisation tricks: his price is high but in line with the standard price list; he can't make the concession you are asking for because it's against company policy; he knows your price is too high from experience with other suppliers; his lawyers will not permit him to modify that punitive clause in the contract.

Such statements are difficult to challenge without appearing rude; that is why they are successful; that is why win:lose players like using them. Don't be rude, but be alert – and don't make concessions based on untruthful statements from across the table.

Sources of mistrust: 2

You're imagining it.

It is important to be alert to dirty tricks. On the other hand, if you make a habit of seeing deception where none exists, you will find it hard to succeed as a win:win negotiator (> > *Yourself*, page 13).

Sources of mistrust: 3

Different frameworks of truth and falsehood.

The Irish, they say, will often tell you what they think you want to hear: 'It's just a step down the road now, you can't miss it', when in fact you are hopelessly lost in the bog.

A Colombian might bring his native horse-trading games to the negotiating table, and bend the truth a little just to spice things up.

In Russia there is a grand old tradition called *vranyó*, where the speaker tells tall stories, knowing very well his audience can catch him out at any time – just for the thrill of courting embarrassment. (In case you think we are being politically incorrect > > *Culture*, page 49.)

Sources of mistrust: 4

Communication problem; garbled messages.

This happens all the time, and especially under negotiating pressure. (> > *Handling the process*, page 113; *Talking and listening*, page 139; *Language*, page 153.)

Sources of mistrust: 5

There's something else wrong.

If you get an uneasy feeling from your opponent's behaviour, don't immediately assume you are being lied to. When reading sub-verbal signals, it can be hard to disentangle the aggressive from the anxious, the embarrassed from the secretive. People often transfer their emotions across from Issue A to Issue B – without even knowing they are doing it. Have you ever met the manager who has a bad meeting at nine o'clock, and shouts down your excellent proposals at ten thirty? Or the teenager who can't tidy her room up because her new haircut doesn't suit her?

Your opponent is squirming in his seat and avoiding your direct gaze. Perhaps he is worried about some bad news he has to break to you in the next half hour. Maybe he's taken a big risk with a concession he granted you earlier, and now he's regretting it. There's even a chance he's gasping for a cigarette but can't see an ashtray on your desk.

Overleaf we offer a step-by-step diagnostic and action plan.

IF YOU'RE BEGINNING TO MISTRUST YOUR OPPONENT

Follow these steps in this order:

Ask general questions and check his answers against what you know: is he willing to have open and honest discussions, or is he evasive? With this in mind,

Ask detailed questions about things he might be concealing or just failing to mention: is he deceiving you in this negotiation? If not, fine. If he is,

Give him an escape route: 'If you have any doubts about what you said before, now is the time to change it . . .' If that doesn't do the trick,

Ask if there's something else wrong: 'I feel you're uncomfortable about something; is there anything you'd like to clarify?' If there is something, deal with it. Otherwise,

Express your misgivings: 'The facts as I see them don't bear out what you are telling me . . .', and

Emphasise the dangers of detection: 'We must suspend this negotiation while we check a few things out. After that, we'll decide whether to back out/get in touch with your superiors/call the Fraud Squad . . .', then

Offer the escape route again: 'We all make mistakes. It's not too late to tell us about any doubts you may have . . .'. If he comes clean,

Pin your opponent down, by getting all concrete details on paper.

8

CREATIVE BARGAINING

'I always end up in a price haggle'

Bargaining over price is part of many negotiations. In different kinds of dealing, it occupies a greater or lesser part of our attention. Sometimes price *is* the overriding factor.

COMMODITY DEALING, HAGGLING AND POWER PLAYS

❑ If you are buying or selling commodities by telephone, price is all you are discussing: 'Quote me for so much coffee/so many pork bellies.' If you like the price you hear, you say 'yes'. If you don't, you say 'no' and call somebody else. This isn't even haggling.

❑ If you are buying a carpet in the souk, and the merchant has established that you like the one he's sitting on, an ancient haggling game begins at which he will almost certainly beat you (> > *Ritual*, page 43). As a general rule of thumb here, if he says 10, he's allowing space to drop to 8, and he really would settle for 6 – so it's worth 4. Offer 2 for openers. The theatrical performance that follows may be very enjoyable – to the point where you concede a few extra pounds as a thank you for the entertainment (> > *Emotion*, page 26) – but it won't really be a creative bargaining session.

❑ If you are negotiating the sale of a job lot of water-damaged carpets after a warehouse fire, the haggling will operate on similar lines, with a few power plays thrown in: 'That's my best offer and I have a train to catch ... Do you have any idea how many fire sales I go to in a year? I *know* what this stuff is worth ... I can just see the look on your boss's face when you go back empty-handed ...'

Commodity dealers do not consider themselves to be negotiators.

The trader in the souk prides himself on his haggling skills, but his act runs along narrow traditional grooves.

The fire sale might be better run as an auction, if you can find more than one potential purchaser: otherwise if it's one-on-one it soon turns into a single-issue negotiation, at which point it's down to sabre-rattling, chest-beating and moral blackmail.

The wise and experienced negotiator will do all he can to avoid becoming embroiled in a single-issue negotiation – including sending muggins in to do it for him: 'Sell those ruined carpets to Mr Barracuda, and don't accept a penny less than £5,000 . . .'

PRICE: THE STICKIEST ISSUE

Inexperienced negotiators are often nervous about being the first to name a ball-park price, perhaps through fear of tragic error.

There is another very good reason for nervousness: once the price debate begins, it is difficult to be free and creative. And if you are negotiating with a win:lose-style opponent, you must beware of 'salami' tactics – shaving slices off your proposal until there is nothing left to negotiate except price, and then insisting that you cut slice after slice off that. So before you reach that stage, you should:

❑ Prepare the ground for a creative bargaining session.
❑ Be ready to resist your opponent's attempts at salami tactics.

Creative bargaining: Ploy 1

Introduce more variables.

Pure price negotiations are quite rare in modern business; you can explore currency exchange rates, credit terms, finance packages, payment by instalments, part-exchange or barter, bulk discounts and many other factors which cluster around the idea of money.

Concerning the goods and services on offer, you should also try to be creative: accept less fancy packaging? travel in the low season? make a three-year commitment? introduce a friend? The list is very long when you start to think about it, and you should think about it well in advance.

Creative bargaining: Ploy 2

Play the fruit machine of variables.

The good old mechanical one-arm bandits had three spinning reels of fruit symbols. If you came up cherry–orange–cherry, you could put another coin in, *hold* the two sets of cherries, and *spin* the orange reel in the hopes of getting three cherries in a row – a winning line.

Play your multi-variable negotiation the same way. Say to your opponent:

> Let's stay with a hypothetical price of £17.30 (*hold*), and suppose that we're going to sign a two-year supply contract (*hold*). We still have to agree on payment terms. Our normal arrangement is 60 days after delivery, but what if we played with that a little? (*spin*).

If that doesn't work, you can put in another coin and spin the whole lot again.

Creative bargaining: Ploy 3

Explore needs and priorities.

If you want to step to your opponent's side and see things from his point of view – with all the negotiating advantages which that will bring – then the best thing is to *ask*. Ask about *his* needs, *his* priorities, *his* hopes, fears, and ambitions. People really do love talking about themselves. (You should have done this at an early stage of the negotiation, but it's never too late to learn more.)
Say:

> I had thought I understood your price limits, and I really believed we could reach an agreement. Perhaps if we looked a bit more closely at your budgetary constraints, and what you really hope to get for your money, we could find another approach.

Then keep asking: 'Why? . . . Have you ever tried another way? . . . Are you sure you're shopping for the right thing?'

Creative bargaining: Ploy 4

Find new linkages and trade-offs.

The idea of negotiating the package recurs again and again in this book; the mark of the creative negotiator is his ability to find new linkages within the package and exploit them (>> *Planning*, page 73; *Handling the process*, page 113; *Movement*, page 128).

Creativity is seldom truly original. Most artists offer a fresh synthesis of what has gone before, filtered through their own vision. Most scientific inventions occur when the inventor pulls together a number of newly developed technologies and finds a fresh application.

Synthesise, pull together, find new linkages. Say:

> It seems to me that you're hampered on price because you're spending too much on transport from the docks to your factory gate. If we could find a way to get those costs down for you, would you be prepared to offer us a little more for the machines? And perhaps we can let you have a disk of the instruction manuals, and you can print your own. What we save on paper and labour we could pass on to you in a slight price reduction. Now the mention of instruction manuals leads us back to the question of operator training.

Creative bargaining: Ploy 5

Find a fresh entry point.

The longer you negotiate within the same industry, over the same product or service, with opponents from the same field, the more you are in danger of getting stuck in a rut.

Take yourself off on a creative thinking course, and apply the results to the package you are offering or demanding.

We once met a purchaser, and observed his treatment of a salesman:

> I have been organising these conferences for twenty years, and I know exactly what I want: a dark blue plastic wallet for the delegates to carry their papers in, overprinted with the logo of the conference, for which I will supply the block. Now, tell me your prices for 5,000, 10,000 and 20,000. We pay 60 days after delivery.

He enjoyed life a lot more once he learned to say:

> Imagine you're a delegate at one of my conferences. What would you like to find in your welcome pack?

or:

> Let's say I have a budget of £10 per delegate for goodies of various kinds. How do you think I should spend the money?

or:

> What ways do you have for the delegates to keep their papers in order?

Creative bargaining: Ploy 6

Play around with time – the most elastic variable.

If people tend to get tense when they talk about cash they are often much more relaxed when you discuss rescheduling, staggering the work to fit the end-customer's project plan, just-in-time delivery, or delivering all the red candles in time for Christmas, and the other colours early in the New Year.
Say:

> I know it's valuable to you to be able to book your workload ahead. Now, if I could find a way to guarantee you a certain minimum of work in the spring months, might you be able to lower your price for the first phase in December–March? You

could buy all your materials now, while prices are low. And perhaps we could split the payments as if it were two separate projects. That way, you would still be getting your final milestone payments on Phase I, as the first money was coming in for Phase II – giving your cash flow a shot in the arm at the end of the tax year. Of course, that's quite a hassle for us, so in return we'd be asking you to get the messy work at the front of the building completed a bit quicker.

Creative bargaining: Ploy 7

Use relationship as a variable.

This does not mean irritating your opponent with a lot of tired old nonsense about 'Since you're such a good customer . . .' or 'I wouldn't make this offer to just anybody . . .' or even 'Tell you what, I like your face, so I'm going to do you a big favour today . . .'

It is, however, quite reasonable to say:

I might be tempted to pay the price you're asking just to get this out of the way and turn my attention to the next job. But some time in the next year, I'm going to be looking for this sort of service again, and I'll have time to shop around. I'm sure you'd like to be on the list. In fact, if you can get your price to the right level, and do a good job, you have a chance of being the only one on the list. I prefer working with people I know and trust.

Or, conversely,

You're squeezing my margins very tight, and asking me to go even lower. Now, I believe that when you see the service we deliver, you'll be asking for more within a year. By that time we'll know you and your people better, and so we'll be in an even better position to tailor our methods to suit you. At that stage, I don't want to upset the relationship by suddenly hiking my price up to a more realistic level.

In either case, you are using the relationship as a variable: we can make a deal in which the relationship is a long and happy one, and this will have an influence on the price; alternatively, we can ignore the long term human/service/creative alliance, and in that case the price will move in the other direction (>>*Relationships*, page 37).

Creative bargaining: Ploy 8

Emphasise transactional value.

The section on *Emotion* has an explanation of transactional value – the benefit that a person can draw from the negotiation itself: the deal went well, and so I feel good, and that's worth a few pounds of anybody's money.
Say:

> Of course I understand that you want to get a good deal here, and I respect that. Let me just explain once more the benefits in the package I'm offering, and perhaps you'll feel more comfortable with the price we're asking.

Or:

> I know how much you'd like to close this sale, but I also sense that you feel a bit squeezed on price – although I'm convinced you've protected your margins adequately. Let me tell you now that I hadn't intended to move at all on the issue of freight insurance/ spare parts stock/penalty clauses, so you'll be walking out of here with a much better deal than you might have got on a bad day. Congratulations!

Creative bargaining: Ploy 9

Have somebody creative on the team.

Many creative thinkers are also softies. This makes them bad negotiators. On the other hand, some of the most experienced and assertive negotiators are a bit weak in the creative department. Thank Heaven we're all different (>>*People*, page 34).

You can afford to let the creative softy loose on a negotiation, provided he has at least one pair of experienced and assertive hands holding the bridle. The only other rule is that he is not allowed to blurt out his creative idea in front of the opposing team without checking it in advance.

It can be very useful, during a time-out, if your creative partner begins to say:

> It's only a thought, but why don't we offer them a new solution to the transport problem? So far, we've assumed that all the heavy equipment will be held in a depot outside Birmingham, but if you look at the construction sites where the equipment will ultimately be used, you'll see they're dotted all around the country. Now, we might both save money if . . .

Creative bargaining: Ploy 10

Communicate the creativity.

Be open about it. If you are stuck in a counter-productive rut, why not say so?

> I'm very much afraid we might be missing opportunities here . . .

And suggest creative alternatives:

> Let's try a bit of lateral thinking/tear up the rule book/spread our wings and fantasise a bit . . . surely between us we can come up with some new angle/break the mould/find a better way than just haggling over price . . . maybe you have some ideas . . .

9

PLANNING

'I'm afraid of getting things wrong'

In this chapter we will be dealing with the preparation and planning you do before you ever meet your opponent across the negotiating table.

Once the negotiation starts, and you enter the propose > discuss > bargain phases, you will revisit the preparation phase during adjournments and time-outs, adjusting your package in the light of what has gone before (> > *Timetabling*, page 108).

Thorough planning brings more benefits than sparkling performance at the table; 70 per cent of your chances of success lie in good preparation. And if fear of mistakes is your problem, you must do your homework in a way that will reduce your fear. Planning does not mean sitting around worrying yourself into a hole in the ground. It means finding things out, deciding what you want, and designing a strategy and an approach.

THE FIRE TRIANGLE

We learn at school that combustion can only occur if there are

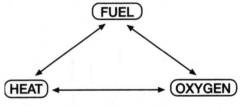

In the same way, effective negotiation can only take place in the presence of:

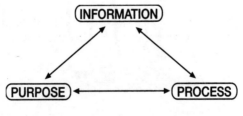

INFORMATION

You are already the world's greatest expert on your own situation. If not, see below: The BATNA and the briefing (page 88).

The most vital information you can gather at the planning stage is to do with your opponent's situation and his interests, and we begin with that.

It is useful to think of this information in two overlapping clusters. Different individuals feel at home in different clusters; X-type people tend to neglect research into Y-type questions – 'it's all too vague/uncomfortable/dangerous'; conversely, those whose working lives centre on Y-type ideas skimp on the X-type questions – 'tedious stuff; leave it to the accountants . . .'

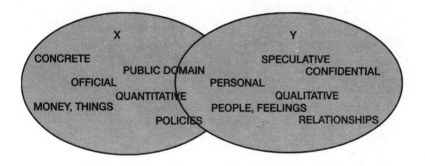

The research you do in Cluster X brings up the sort of information you will put on the table at the official negotiation.

Cluster Y material is more useful in tête-à-tête conversations, and at the dinner/in the sauna/on the golf course.

Both sets of material are vital to the outcome of your negotiation.

WHAT THIS MEANS TO YOU

Take a look at yourself and be honest (> > *Yourself*, page 13).

If you are inclined to overlook or avoid issues in one or the other cluster, either force yourself to get interested, or have somebody on the team whose tastes balance out your distastes.

Information gathering: Step 1

Do all the common sense homework.

Has your company done business with this person or company before? Interview the people who did the deal, the project leaders since then and anybody else who might have a story to tell.

The most important information is to do with your opponent's real priorities, and how they fit with your own. Your negotiation should be aiming for a win:win result. In each trade-off, you try to deliver something of high value to your opponent which costs you little; or you try to extract from him something which costs him little, but means a lot to you (> > *Introduction*, page 10).

So at an early stage you need an idea of how each variable is valued by him/his employer/his institution.

Information gathering: Step 2

List the variables in the negotiation.

These vary widely industry by industry, market by market, deal by deal, but the following might help: it relates to teams of Western specialists negotiating in China for the supply of mobile telephone installations.

CHECKLIST: VARIABLES OF A NEGOTIATION

Basic quality
Fancy trimmings
Ease of implementation
Maintenance
Spare parts
Price
Payment terms
Help with financing
Currency
Transport
Delivery time
Flexible consignments
Guarantees
Steady relationship
Help with project management
Staff training
Quality of documentation
Transfer of technology
Help with promotion/advertising
Volume discount
Options on future business
Publicity
Personal status
Fun

Each one of these breaks down into a sub-set of variables. 'Basic quality' might embrace 'number of coats of paint on the storage racks', 'size of battery for standby operation' and so on; and 'Help with financing' will cover interest rates, drawdown facilities, and a dozen other considerations.

Information gathering: Step 3

Allocate a code letter to each variable, and plot them on one of these graphs:

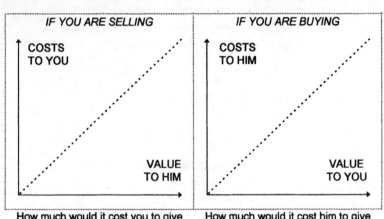

IF YOU ARE SELLING	IF YOU ARE BUYING
COSTS TO YOU / VALUE TO HIM	COSTS TO HIM / VALUE TO YOU
How much would it cost you to give him what he wants, and how important is it to him to get it?	How much would it cost him to give you what you want, and how important is it to you to get it?

Your graph will look like this: or this: or this:

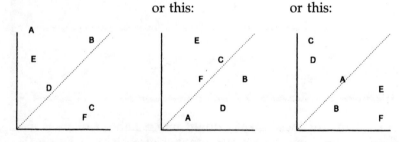

In business negotiations, 'price' normally comes out on the dotted line: cash is usually a zero-sum game. If the seller drops his price by a dollar, that shift is worth precisely a dollar to the buyer. Hence the dogmatic atmosphere which often prevails in price-only deals (> > *Creative bargaining*, page 63).

The items that cluster round the bottom right-hand corner are often very interesting. In many negotiations, they are matters relating to personal satisfaction and relationships. In recent years, as costs have been cut to the bone, and markets become saturated, sellers have sought an extra something they can give their customers without driving their price up – a smile, air miles, a customer charter.

TEN THINGS YOUR OPPONENT WANTS

1. To feel good about himself.
2. Not to feel bullied.
3. A lasting alliance.
4. To know and understand more.
5. To finish the negotiation without working too hard.
6. Money, goods and services.
7. To be treated nicely – particularly to be listened to.
8. To be liked.
9. Clear communication.
10. Recognition of his ability and effort – from you, his boss, his colleagues.

Notice this: only item 6 on the list actually costs you anything to deliver.

Information gathering: Step 4

Look for trade-offs, sticking points and areas of ignorance.

Say:
   'Clearly we can offer to share the costs on item E . . .'
   'Then if we can persuade him to lose a bit of money by moving on D, we can repay him handsomely by conceding A.'
   '. . . or at least it'll seem handsome to him. We can't afford to move on B – unless he comes up with something dramatic on C.'

'Or C and F somehow linked . . .'
'We really don't know how he sees the issue of F. We must ask about that during the agenda discussion.'
'Fine. But whatever happens, we must protect our interests on B.'

Write the linked items down on an IF. . .THEN . . . list like this. (Once again, the first line is an example.)

IF. . .	THEN . . .
* . . . they agree to pay freight insurance	* . . . we'll set generous payment terms
*	*
*	*
*	*
*	*
*	*

You will find new opportunities for trade-offs once the negotiation starts, and this list will be much amended before it finishes (> > *Movement*, page 129).

WHAT THIS MEANS TO YOU

In your efforts to avoid 'getting it wrong', the most useful thing you can do is try to work out your opponent's priorities: where's the end of *his* rainbow?; What kind of monkey does he have on *his* back? What will he see as a positive outcome — realistically?

Then check his priorities against your own, and start meshing the two.

PURPOSE

After 'information', 'purpose' is the second apex of the fire triangle. This does not at all mean that you gather all the information and *then* start thinking about your purpose. From the word go you should be asking yourself and others:

❑ Why are you getting into this negotiation?
❑ What do you hope to bring out of it – realistically?
❑ How will you distinguish between success and failure?

It is really a question of clarification and commitment: clear your mind as to what you really want – bearing in mind that you can't have everything – and tell yourself that you're going to do your best to get it. Most mistakes come from a lack of focus.

Focussing your purpose: 1

Decide: a quick fix or a long-term relationship?

Sometimes we do business only once with a given opponent. Neither the tourist haggling in the street market nor the couple buying a flat expect a lasting business relationship with the vendor. The Wall Street corporate raider fully expects his victim to be upset afterwards.

Conversely (and more commonly in business), you might be seeing your negotiation as part of a longer relationship, or as one step in the development of a market area, or as a crucial element in a bigger programme of business. In that case, you will stress the variables that contribute to the grand design, and be more modest about short-term financial gain (>> *Targets*, page 91).

WHAT THIS MEANS TO YOU

Make sure that you and everybody on your side has a clear view of your purpose expressed in simple terms that everybody can understand and remember:

'We want lots of money fast/we want these goods as cheap as we can get them/we must sell this whole batch at one go before it rots on the quayside'

or

'We want this business for more than just money reasons/we want the prestige of dealing with this client/small profits now will lead to big business later.'

Focusing your purpose: 2

For each of your variables, work out:

1. *The best you might possibly get – realistically.*
2. *The worst you could consider – any worse, you'd walk away.*
3. *The acceptable median – a feel-good result.*

THE RANGE OF OUTCOMES

If a negotiation reaches a result, then each side, with respect to each variable factor, should be able to say:

1. 'It was the best that we could have hoped for, given that the other side had ambitious targets and made no silly mistakes.'
2. 'It was a worst case result for us. Any worse, and we'd have walked away from the table.'
3. 'We found an acceptable median on this one; there was good and bad elsewhere in the package, but on this variable we came out OK.'

The grid below will help you map out the target range for each variable. The first line is an example, seen from the point of view of a price-sensitive buyer.

NB: The *acceptable* entry is not just an arithmetical average of the other two.

YOUR BARGAINING RANGE

VARIABLE:	BEST	ACCEPTABLE	WORST
e.g. *Price/kilo*	£35.75	£41.50	£44.00
1.			
2.			
3.			
etc			

This will be one of the key pieces of paper in your case (or files on your disk) when the negotiation begins.

WHAT THIS MEANS TO YOU

If you're forced into *worst* on a given issue, you'll want *best* on something else, as a compensation.

Focusing your purpose: 3

Work out the costs of possible concessions.

For example:

If you are bearing the costs of transport, how much would it cost you to provide an extra truck for deliveries in peak periods?

If you are buying machines for resale, and your supplier asks you to assemble them in your own warehouse, what would the bill be for wages, insurance, factory overheads?

If you are selling chemicals, remember that a 2 per cent discount for a bulk order might cost you less than 2 per cent, if you could buy your own materials cheaper and save on storage – work it out.

You can note these hypothetical costs to line up with the grid you have already made (see facing page).

WHAT THIS MEANS TO YOU

Once the negotiation begins, you might react in emotional ways to some of your opponent's suggestions: 'He's being greedy! Damned if I'll say yes to that!' At such times, you will need the support of the cool calculations you made during the planning stage.

PROCESS

Your work on 'purpose' and 'information' can go on simultaneously. Once you have clear goals and adequate knowledge, you can work out a route to where you want to be.

In our experience, most negotiators focus a great deal on the results or business outcomes of a negotiation, and shy away from the actual process. If you take the initiative, and have ideas to offer, you can find yourself in the driving seat – with all the

VARIABLE:	BEST	ACCEPTABLE	WORST	COST OF CONCESSIONS:
1. Transport	Five of our trucks, seven at peak	Six of our trucks, seven at peak	Rent eighth truck for peak periods	£550 per day, inclusive
2. Assembly	Assembled; we pay basic wage costs	Assembled; we pay costs plus margin	Kit delivery: assembly by our staff	£120 per machine
3. Discount	No discount	1% for 20 tons; 2% for 50 tons	2% for 20 tons	1.5% – £4.50 per ton
etc.				

responsibilities and advantages that entails. (>>*Handling the process*, page 113).

WHAT THIS MEANS TO YOU

Somebody *had* better think about how to move the business forward. It might as well be *you*.

Setting up the process: Sketchmap 1

Take all the bits so far, and pull them together into a draft agenda.

Spread out on the desk, the screen or the pinboard, you should now have:

- ❑ A list of variables (Step 2 above).
- ❑ A graph of priorities and costs (Step 3 above).
- ❑ An 'If . . . Then . . .' table (Step 4 above).
- ❑ A clear statement of your purpose (Focus 1 above).
- ❑ A bargaining range grid (Focus 2 above).
- ❑ Notes on costs of concessions (Focus 3 above).

You almost have a plan now. You really can't do much more until the talking begins; after all, your opponent has probably been doing something similar, and the discussion phase (>>*Timetabling*, page 108) will permit you to find out how far his plans have advanced, and how they match yours.

THE MAP IS NOT THE TERRITORY

Orienteering is the sport involving maps, compasses, cross-country running, checkpoints and time penalties. It provides several useful analogies when we think about negotiating.

An orienteer is given sight of the course map before the event, and he studies it carefully, identifying the steep rocky bits and the marshy areas, and thinking about the effects of the season.

But he knows that conditions on the day – weather, ground conditions, the tactics of opposing teams – will make the course look very different. And his team will only learn the positions of the checkpoints as the event begins.

So the orienteer cannot make a clear, detailed plan in advance.

Having said that, he will certainly lose if he doesn't work on the map and get a feel for the terrain before he laces up his running shoes.

There is a danger in writing an agenda in advance: you begin to script the meeting in advance, drawing an ideal path for yourself through the items on the list. When the discussion phase starts, you are inflexible, and deaf to any ideas that might upset your 'plan'.

The trick is to visualise the agenda in a non-linear map. Instead of: 1. Scope; 2. Price; 3. Bulk discount; 4. Payment terms; 5. Transport; 6. etc.; 7. etc. you draw something like this:

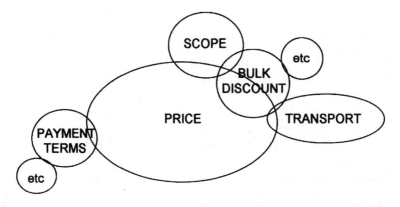

This is one planning document that you can safely let your opponent see. For more about what happens after that, including the production of Sketchmap 2, see *Handling the process*, page 117.

The fire triangle is now complete. You have the relevant information, you know your purpose, and you have paid attention to the process you will follow. Fuel, heat and oxygen. We anticipate a merry blaze.

One more thing to plan for – the sudden downpour of rain that kills the fire. What will you do if the negotiation fails?

THE BATNA AND THE BRIEFING

In their classic *Getting to YES*, Roger Fisher and William Ury coined the term BATNA: Best Alternative to a Negotiated Agreement.

You are not ready for the pressures of negotiation unless you have a clear idea of your escape route. If you become obsessed with the idea of success, and have no idea which way to turn if it collapses, you will be in a weak position – likely to give too much away.

Prepare yourself psychologically (and your team-mates, if you have them), by saying: 'If, through no fault of ours, this goes wrong, it's not the end of the world. We can implement Plan B: our BATNA.'

Participants on negotiation seminars often have difficulty here: they are looking for a PATNA: *Perfect* Alternative to a Negotiated Agreement. It doesn't exist.

Probably the BATNA will involve a sacrifice, a backward step, or a lot of hard work; otherwise, you'd be pursuing your BATNA, rather than get involved in this negotiation. Here are some typical BATNAs: 'If the negotiation fails, we'll:

Scrap x project, and reallocate the budget to an extra sales push.

Buy a machine with fewer facilities.

Dig into our savings, and live on beans on toast for a while.'

All this advice on planning assumes that you are expert in the operations of your own side and fully empowered to make your own decisions in the context of targets you have set for yourself.

Often, of course, you go into a negotiation because you've been told to go. Equally often, the person sending you (your boss?) fails to give you the time, support, guidance, information or freedom of action you would like: you are badly briefed.

A TYPICAL BRIEFING

'Get in there tomorrow and negotiate hard. Don't settle for a penny less than £7.50 a dozen, and make sure they know we're doing them a favour. The file on the last negotiation went missing when Parker left to work for the competition, but it was a sorry catalogue of failure, so you're better off without it. Good luck! I'm off to give the New York office a bad time for a few days . . .'

AND HOW TO PUT IT RIGHT

1. Negotiate for more preparation time. Tomorrow? Ridiculous! Be assertive. Allow plenty of time for the discussion phase with your opponent. You need to do a lot of listening to make up for that lost file.
2. Get your boss's sponsorship: make sure you can use his authority to get all the internal information you need, and quickly.
3. Nail him down to a BATNA – so that anything you negotiate which is more useful than the BATNA will be seen as a success. His £7.50 bottom line is a macho pose.

10

TARGETS

'I worry about not getting the best deal possible'

Not surprisingly, people who are a bit relaxed about their targets often come out with better deals than those who sink their teeth in and worry at the problem like a dog with a rat.

Remember that your opponent is also making preparations, and his plans are unlikely to be a perfect match with yours. That's why you're negotiating. So 'the best deal possible' must mean, in practice, 'a deal I can be satisfied with, and which will leave my opponent satisfied too.' Dead rats are not a useful source of future business.

The setting of targets is a vital stage in preparation, but you must also leave yourself free to make creative moves once the negotiation begins at the table (>> *Creative bargaining*, page 63).

We list here the sort of targets you should *not* set yourself.

Targets to avoid: 1

Woolly hopeless daydreams about some ill-defined future.

'It might be nice if we could find a way to improve the situation, and make a bit more money out of this operation one day. Who knows, we might get really lucky . . .'

If you enter a negotiation with targets like that, you might come out with some sort of deal, but it will be a long way short of 'the best possible'.

Your short-term targets – which relate to the most concrete elements in your package proposal – should be SMART:

Simple, so that everyone can grasp them;
Measurable, so you know how close you are to what you want;
Achievable, by the people involved with the resources to hand;
Realistic, given that your opponent has goals too; and
Timed, as in deadlines, delivery schedules or whatever.

'Dear Rich Uncle Harry, I would like a red mountain bike with 15 gears for my next birthday; I enclose a mail-order catalogue with the relevant page marked.' This is the expression of a SMART target; it is now up to Uncle Harry to impose conditions in the negotiation.

Targets to avoid: 2

Greedy, presumptuous expectations that will shock your opponent.

If you have your opponent trapped, with nowhere else to turn, you might 'succeed' in extracting a painful maximum from him. We don't call that 'negotiation'.

During the Vietnam war, the American, 'doves' mounted a campaign to 'win the hearts and minds of the Vietnamese people', and turn them against the guerrillas. The 'hawks' had a cynical view of the programme: 'When you have them by the balls, their hearts and minds will follow.' The hawks were wrong.

In your negotiation, you should be aiming for the optimum, not the maximum. Of course, you should aim high. If he aims high and you aim low, you won't come out of it well.

A good test of your predetermined targets is this: if your opponent looks you steadily in the eye at the start of the negotiation, and asks: 'What exactly are you hoping to gain from these discussions?', will you be able to look *him* in the eye and state your aims without embarrassment?

If the package you are selling has a value of £8–10, then you should assume your opponent knows that too. If you open at £11.50, he'll probably respond with £6.50, and you'll have a lot of work to do to close the gap. If you open at £14, he'll go £4 – if he can speak at all. No deal.

Research the market; consider the competition; don't treat your opponent like a fool.

Targets to avoid: 3

'Lock-in' objectives that take you past the point of no return.

Macbeth is doing very well in his career until the three witches suggest he might become king. He tells his wife, and she locks him in on the objective by having him murder the present king in his sleep. Tragedy follows.

The targets you set yourself in the planning stage can be psychologically dangerous: you develop a picture in your mind of how good things would be if you got everything you wanted, and very quickly you start thinking of how good things *will* be when you *do* get everything you want.

From there it is only a short step to seeing your targets as your rights, and treating your opponent as an enemy who is trying to deny you what you clearly deserve. Before long, you find yourself saying: 'take it or leave it', or 'that's not negotiable', or 'make my day, punk'. All your opponent will see is pathetic posturing.

Stay realistic about your targets (>> *Planning*, page 82).

Targets to avoid: 4

Purely short-term goals.

Some negotiations are natural one-offs. If you are selling your house to a stranger, you will probably go for bust.

Otherwise, when you are considering 'What will constitute the best deal possible?', you should be including such factors as: options on future business; your reputation in the market as a good person to do business with; strengthening the relationship with your client (>> *Raising the game*, page 97; *Relationships*, page 37).

Quite likely the boss who briefs you for the negotiation will fail to include such factors: 'There's a cash-flow panic this quarter: for God's sake bring home the bacon!' Use your powers of persuasion (>> *Talking and listening*, page 146) to convince him that 'soft' factors are also important (>> *Planning*, page 75).

Targets to avoid: 5

Hard position statements.

The targets you express – Simple, Measurable, Achievable, Realistic, Timed – are only the outward expression of your deeper needs.

If we take the mountain bike example above, Rich Uncle Harry would be quite within his rights to ask: 'Why do you want this birthday present?' The answer might be 'to get to and from school and do a newspaper delivery round', or 'to be just like the other guys', or even 'to be one up on the other guys'. It isn't good enough for his nephew just to say: 'because I want it!'

In your negotiation, you should be measuring the 'best deal possible' not against the positions you adopt in the statement of your targets, but against your deeper needs – getting a more pleasant place to live at a price you can afford; finding a way to get your products established in a new market; convincing your blue-collar staff to begin accepting a performance-related pay scheme.

If the deal you negotiate deviates in some details from your initial target, that doesn't mean you've failed – provided it serves the underlying purpose.

DON'T SAY	**SAY RATHER**
We desperately want to get X.	We desperately want to achieve A, B, C. X would be one way of doing so.

Targets to avoid: 6

Our side 7; their side 0.

This is a target to set in competitive sport, or in total warfare – not in a negotiation.

If there are seven variables in your negotiation package, with room for a bit of give-and-take on each variable, then you should be aiming for healthy trade-offs, not the obliteration of all your opponent's hopes in a seven-nil wipeout (>> *Creative bargaining*, page 63).

Ideally, you should come out feeling you've done well on four or five out of the seven – and your opponent should be feeling that he has done well on four or five out of seven – win:win (>> *Introduction*, page 10).

DON'T SAY	SAY RATHER
We want to get X out of them.	We want to get X from them, perhaps in return for Y from us.

WHAT THIS MEANS TO YOU

Your targets should be:

1. SMART, so you really know what you're aiming for.
2. Optimal, and recognisable as such by your opponent.
3. Flexible, so you don't get obsessive.
4. Long-term, if there are long-term possibilities.
5. Linked to your overarching strategies or deeper needs.
6. Generous to your opponent, within reasonable limits.

11

RAISING THE GAME

'The competition is cheaper/quicker/better than us'

In a simple sales situation, negotiation about price, speed of delivery or technical quality never takes place: the premiums on health insurance are fixed by the actuaries according to your age and medical history; the delivery arrangements on the *Golden Universe Encyclopedia* are not up for discussion ('allow 28 days after order'); the specification and performance of the vacuum cleaner are engineered in before it leaves the factory.

If you want to sell insurance, encyclopedias or vacuum cleaners, buy a book about selling. This is a book about negotiating.

In a complex sale, it is the job of the salesman to clear a way to the table for the sales negotiator, who then goes in to get the best feasible deal.

If you, as a sales negotiator, feel weak by comparison with the competition, then ask yourself one question: 'If our competitors are cheaper, quicker and better, why is this purchaser still interested in our offer?'

Raising the game has nothing to do with getting greedy; if you feel your competitors are stronger than you, it is a bad time to try grabbing a bigger short-term profit. Raising the game means playing for higher stakes in the 'soft' areas – what you can do for your opponent in terms of service, relationship, personal growth, long-term benefits and ethical behaviour.

Game-raising strategy 1

Recognise the complexity of your opponent's requirements.

In the competitive situation described, you feel enfeebled. You are supposed to push through the negotiation to reach your company's goals (a profitable sale), but you fear the force of your opponent's arguments against you:

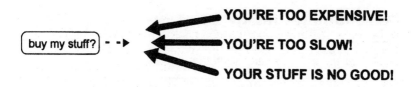

In fact, your opponent is a complex human being with complex needs, and his view of the situation embraces many factors – complementary, contradictory and personal to him, or his team:

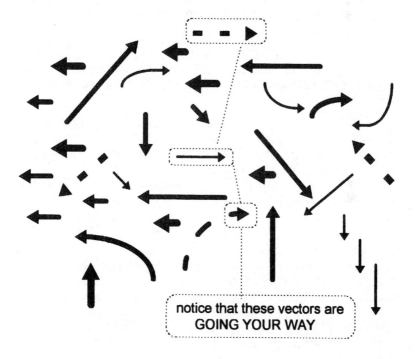

The trick is first to find those minor vectors in your opponent's complex make-up that move in a direction to suit you. Then you boost these vectors in importance, until they influence his whole perception of the deal.

Game-raising strategy 2

Teach him the value of your strengths in other areas.

Say:

> We can't beat Co. X on price or speed of delivery. (I know their warehouse is full at the moment, since they overestimated demand . . .)
>
> Their new model has one or two features that ours lacks. (Once we are convinced of the value of these features, we will offer them too – and one or two real eye-openers which we're working on right now . . .)
>
> But I'd really like to show one or two areas where our package is strong – areas which are important to you. I'm on a straight salary as a customer support engineer – unlike some of the people you've been talking to, who depend on sales commission to make their living.

These 'minor' vectors will often be connected with 'soft' or abstract ideas. If your opponent usually thinks in concrete commercial terms, when you address these ideas you will be telling him something *unfamiliar*.

It is difficult to get people to understand abstract, unfamiliar ideas. All kinds of teachers have faced this problem, and come up with the same answer: you have to translate your abstract, unfamiliar proposition into terms which are concrete and familiar to your student.

Travelling salesmen carry cases of samples and photographic pamphlets. Their tubes of toothpaste or their toothpaste-making machines are concrete enough, but they are unfamiliar to the customer. He won't buy until he has at least seen them, and preferably touched them, so that they become familiar. Then he can understand and remember the commercial benefits.

The vicar's sermon is usually on a standard theological theme – an abstract idea, which will be quite familiar to his congregation. It is his job to bring the idea to life, and help his flock to absorb the spiritual benefits. To do so he must express the abstract in terms of the concrete. He relies heavily on symbols –

the Lamb, the Cross, the Trinity – and he tells simple stories about fishermen, soldiers, rich men, poor men, prodigal sons and wise virgins.

The American management consultant working in the post-communist world (or the Jesuit missionary up the Orinoco) has a double problem to solve: his ideas are both abstract and unfamiliar. He sometimes makes the mistake of offering concrete examples from an unfamiliar world, which only confuses the client further: what can an Albanian make of a metaphor based on a California lifestyle (or what can a jungle Indian make of the story of the loaves and fishes)?

The only route from abstract/unfamiliar to the zone of real communication lies through the abstract/familiar quadrant. To explain the unfamiliar abstract of acceleration, the physics

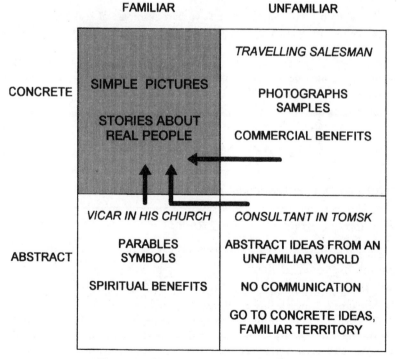

Where real communication happens

teacher combines two abstracts which the pupils are already comfortable with: speed and time. Then he begins to talk about dropping cannon-balls from the Leaning Tower, and the performance of drag racers. There is no point in describing the actions of particles and waves which the pupils have never encountered before.

WHAT THIS MEANS TO YOU

Your customer has needs over and above short-term commercial gain, and you can negotiate about those needs.

Such ideas might be new to him, and seem like pie in the sky.

Draw simple sketches for him. Give him examples of real people, in situations he will recognise, who have gained real benefit from the ideas you are explaining.

When your ideas are concrete and familiar, he will see their importance.

Game-raising strategy 3

Focus on long-term gain and personal satisfaction.

Combining Strategies 1 and 2, say:

You might make a decision based simply on price, availability and apparent technical superiority – and regret it 18 months from now when your whole system needs an upgrade. We like to think we offer a future-proof service and a working relationship that will see you through good years and bad years.

There's a client of ours just down the road – Acme Engineering by the traffic lights – who switched to another supplier three years ago, and found that he couldn't help them with the system modification they wanted a year after that. The supplier was term deal, but he didn't have the back-up engineering staff to offer a tailored solution. Acme came back to us and we sorted them out pronto.

I'd like to show you how our customer support service works – perhaps even invite you down to look around and meet one or two of our people over lunch. The decision will be yours, of course, but I think you'll probably see the advantages. I'd like you to be making a choice you'll be comfortable with three years from now.

Game-raising strategy 4

Make the cake bigger.

50 per cent of 150 is better than 60 per cent of 120.

If your competitor is offering a 1000 lawnmowers, in kit form, FOB Felixstowe, and you can't beat his price, speed or quality, offer the customer 1000 machines, fully assembled, CIF at his warehouse in New Jersey – and a set of tools with every mower (the cherry on top of the cake). If your package is good enough, he might order 2000.

You will, of course, build into your overall price the extra cost of assembly, shipping and insurance, and the toolkit. But the money you charge for these extras doesn't have to give you a margin of profit, and so you are offering your customer a real bargain on assembly, delivery and extra goodies. Meanwhile you've protected the profit margin on the lawnmowers them-selves (> >*Movement*, page 134).

Game-raising strategy 5

Be very honest, very open; go up an ethical level.

Different cultures have different tolerance levels for 'knocking the competition'; it is common in the USA for Ice-Cream Joe to go on TV and say 'Our sundaes have gooier sauce than Freezer

Freddy's', while in Germany such practices are legally danger-ous.

In this competitive negotiation, you might be tempted to say:

> If Co. X are offering you such a low price, they must be using low-grade raw materials/dumping last season's surplus stock/getting ready to go out of business . . . and I've heard rumours that their digital wobulator goes rusty if you leave it out in the rain.

Think twice before you get into this game: your customer might smile and nod, but he's simultaneously making a mental note: 'If this guy stoops this low when he comes under a bit of competitive pressure, he might not be the kind of business partner I want.'

Better to put yourself in the other bracket. Say:

> I can see how you must be tempted by Co. X's offer. Since you've found the time to see me today, I must assume there is something in our approach that you like. Maybe we won't do business this time around, but I'd like to think you'll be back, so I'm available now to answer any questions you might have about our products and services, our plans for the future, and the way we like to work with our clients. If you have questions I can't answer, I'll find the answers.

You can sometimes reinforce your status as Mr Good Guy by steering the conversation into areas like the environment ('We use at least 35 per cent recycled materials, and the emissions are well inside EU regulations . . .'), staff welfare and safety ('We use an earth connection screwed to the chassis; our competitor's soldered connection is probably fine, but I'd hate to be the one switching on in the morning if it had worked loose . . .'), and your readiness to go further than just honouring the contract ('Acme Engineering were particularly pleased that we got to them within 24 hours, although technically the call-out arrange-ment had lapsed . . .').

The impetus for firms to qualify for BS5750, ISO 9000, *Investor In People* status, and similar schemes is precisely so that they can come to any negotiating table with their credentials officially supported: we are a well-organised, ethical company, with more in mind than simple short-term material gain.

Game-raising strategy 6

Purchasing? Procurement? Or strategic alliance?

Many traditional purchasing departments are now shifting the emphasis to the more modern idea of procurement. One difference is that the buyer now involves himself more in the supplier's business affairs: he doesn't just want the goods to arrive at the factory gate on time, he wants to know how they got there, how they were made in the first place, what value the supplier has added during manufacture, and so on. This connects with the ideas of ethical partnership suggested in Strategy 5 above.

The next step is the idea of the strategic alliance, in which the purchaser and supplier find a way to share management responsibility and risk:

> These contracts you have with us have grown to 27 per cent of your turnover: shouldn't we set up a business together for handling this work?
>
> We get you as a secure supplier at a fair price; you get us as a secure purchaser who will put you at the top of the list for future business. We share the risks, we share the profits, we develop policy and strategy together.

The purchasing manager's motto has always been 'Keep your supplier lean but alive'. For a strategic partner, it might be amended to: 'Keep your supplier happy and healthy in any way you can while he does the same for you'.

The idea connects with the currently fashionable idea of stakeholding: primitive competitive capitalism is seen as wasteful and destructive, while communism is clearly a dud. If capitalist companies negotiate openly together, and share an interest in satisfying each others' stakeholders – customers, shareholders, bankers, staff, suppliers, neighbours and no doubt tax inspectors – then society will get all the benefits in efficiency and quality that come from a free market, with less of the unpleasant fallout – redundancies, bankruptcies, corruption, illness through stress and pollution.

If you are already negotiating at this level, all the first five strategies for raising the game must be familiar to you. Most readers of this 'How to . . .' book are probably operating at a more simple level.

But if, at your simple level of negotiation, you find that the traditional variables of price, speed and quality are working against you, try working sequentially through strategies 1–6 until you find a new working relationship with your opponent – *at a higher level of the game.*

12

TIMETABLING

'I'm always too busy and the deal gets made in a rush'

The first piece of advice is quite obvious.

Timetabling: Rule 1

Slow things down.

If the rush is your own fault, then go on a course, or read a book, to improve your time management skills. There are no techniques on offer for 'How to succeed as a lightning negotiator', or 'Shoot-from-the-hip negotiating'. You must find time to negotiate well. *Slow things down.*

If your boss is loading too much work on you, and asking you to negotiate in a hurry, select one of the persuasion tools from *Talking and listening*, page 146 and convince him that you need more time to *slow things down.*

If your opponent is in a great hurry, you have a choice – either take advantage of his haste and so screw a better deal out of him (only in a 'quick fix'/win:lose negotiation), or educate him in the importance of *slowing things down.*

If he is only pretending to be in a hurry in order to put pressure on you, consider the lessons in *Handling the process*, page 113.

Timetabling: Rule 2

Abide by the four phases.

Several chapters in this book deal in depth with the work at various stages: *Planning* and *Targets* are about the preparation phase, and *Creative bargaining* and *Movement* are obviously to do with what comes later.

You will find other books, courses and training videos which talk about the six stages, or the three activities, or the seven pillars of wisdom. It doesn't really matter what we call them. Here we have called them the four phases.

In this chapter we are mainly concerned with not jumping around between phases, and making sure you perform thoroughly the activities of Phase 2, say, before you move on to Phase 3.

For example: don't get stuck into detailed haggling over details before you've got the big picture, and before you've established a good, equal working relationship with your opponent.

We offer here a generalised checklist of the four phases. We strongly recommend you devise one of your own – directly relevant to the business you are in, and personal to you. If you have team-mates, get them together for a couple of hours and work through this list, saying: 'What does this mean to us in concrete terms, and how are we going to live up to this plan in our next negotiation?'

PREPARATION

❑ What do we want to achieve?
❑ How good is our information about them, and their goals?
❑ What do we know about the competition?
❑ What will our proposals cost us; what are they worth to them?
❑ What are the trade-off values of our planned concessions?
❑ If we're in a team, how will we divide the work up?
❑ Have we got a good place for the meetings?

DISCUSSION

❑ We make sure we're negotiating with the right people.
❑ We use the agenda session to learn their priorities.
❑ We listen, watch and ask questions.
❑ We enrich the discussion with new variables.
❑ We are alert for signs of deviousness on their part.
❑ We do not hurry under pressure; we play for time.
❑ We offer to take responsibility for the process.

PROPOSALS

❑ We don't move until we have their complete shopping list.
❑ We make hypothetical trade-offs: 'If you would . . ., then I might . . .'
❑ We check understanding – summaries and loops.
❑ We call for time-outs so we can re-package our offer.
❑ Our attitude and expressions are always positive.
❑ We take them into account as people with people-needs.
❑ We listen carefully to their proposals and probe with questions.

BARGAINING

❑ We aim for a bilateral good deal – win:win.
❑ We keep our fall-back position (BATNA) always in mind.
❑ We play with variables and linkages within the package.
❑ We carefully check the cost of each offer and counter-offer.
❑ We double-check the detail, by comparing notes.
❑ We make sure the final result is:

  ❑ the best alternative;
  ❑ tenable, fair and legal;
  ❑ simple to explain to those involved in carrying it out.

❑ We follow up on the agreement.

Timetabling: Rule 3

Allow time for reiteration.

We have said that it is important to stick to the running order suggested by the four-phase model.

But what happens if, during the discussion phase, you learn something new about your opponent, which drastically changes the decisions you made during the preparation phase? Well then you do go back.

Say:

> We've learnt a lot from this initial discussion, and I think an adjournment would be useful . . .

Then you adjust your plan in the light of what you have learned – with time and space to think clearly (> > *Handling the process*, page 121).

Timetabling: Rule 4

Be patient, but don't overtax your opponent's patience.

NEGOTIATION TIME BUDGET

The first half of the negotiation takes 80 per cent of the time.
The second half of the negotiation takes 80 per cent of the time.

Don't slow things down too much, and don't go round the reiterative loop too many times. Sooner or later you will need to make decisions and move on to the next negotiation. Listen to your impulses (> > *Emotion*, page 29).

THE FABLE OF THE MAGIC FISH

A poor man went out fishing one day, and he cast his line in an inlet of the lake where he had never tried his luck before. He caught a talking fish.

The fish said, 'Before you return me to the water, you may ask me to grant three wishes, but please be quick!'

The poor man lay the gasping fish in the bottom of the boat and started to think about all the lovely things he might wish for.

When he looked again, the fish was dead.

13

HANDLING THE PROCESS

'I hate working under pressure'

Pressure and process: 1

You have to live with a bit of pressure.

Of course there are always pressures and stresses in a negotiation, almost by definition. Without them, a negotiation becomes a formless and pointless gossip session. Correctly handled, these shaping forces can help bring about a successful outcome – just as stage fright, an apparently negative factor, can energise an actor into a winning performance.

If you cannot enjoy a normal healthy level of pressure in your negotiation, you need to work on willpower and a proper sense of proportion; otherwise, *if you can't stand the heat, get out of the kitchen* (> > *Yourself*, page 13).

WHAT THIS MEANS TO YOU	
DON'T SAY	**SAY RATHER**
It can't be done I can't afford to fail. My opponent is out to crush me.	We're aiming high. This is my chance to shine. My opponent has goals of his own.

If you are expecting the pressure to reach abnormal, unhealthy levels, then your powers of conflict handling will be put to the test. (> > *Truth*, page 61; *Talking and listening*, page 150).

If you are untroubled by self-doubt, then the pressure you experience must be coming from your opponent, or from the process of negotiation itself.

'Pressure' is one metaphor for the cause of discomfort. You might equally well say 'Things are moving too fast for me'.

PROVERBS TO CONTEMPLATE

Marry in haste, repent at leisure
Look before you leap
Fools rush in where angels fear to tread

In *Planning* we stress the importance of a calm and ordered preparation period. Calm and order are just as important when the planning is over and the negotiating process begins.

Pressure and process: 2

Set the right ground rules; establish the right atmosphere.

It's very useful if you can be the one to set the ground rules for the process: that means you can build in calm, space and order from the beginning.

If you are hosting the negotiation, you should give some thought to setting the atmosphere and dressing the stage.

Make your guests feel they are welcome, without being too hospitable: if you cover them in kindness at the beginning they will feel uncomfortable: 'If we accept this generosity now will we compromise our bargaining position tomorrow?'

Your faxes and phone calls during the run-up should be polite, timely, efficient and considerate. Your opponent will probably feel compelled to respond in the same manner.

Offer help, if appropriate, with immigration/local transport/ accommodation/communication arrangements. Let the other side know what the timetable will look like, and who will be on your team.

Prepare a room for the negotiation. Ideally, there should be a rectangular table across which the two sides can face each other, with space for papers to be spread and calculators to be deployed; an area for informal mingling (lounge chairs around the coffee pot, perhaps); and a place for your opponents to take time-outs undisturbed. Whiteboards, pinwalls and flipcharts are all very useful. Have the rooms pleasantly lit, with a supply of refreshments laid on. Vases of roses aren't necessary, but neither are smelly ashtrays left over from yesterday's sales meeting.

Pressure and process: 3

Create a nice spacious agenda.

Again, if you are the host (or customer), you will have the right to suggest rules for the negotiation: pistols at dawn, a quiet game of poker, or a gentlemanly discussion aimed at finding an amicable solution? (We prefer the latter.)

If you are the visitor (or seller), your host might feel he should be the one to decide procedures – especially if he represents a rigidly bureaucratic company, or is spending government money, or is acting on behalf of a third party to an agreed brief.

In such cases, you will probably have to accept the letter of the rules as your opponent lays them down – he probably hasn't got the authority to change them. (Anyway, if you manage to make any agreements outside the rules, those agreements will be untenable later, and you will both have wasted your time.)

In general, the visitor/seller accepts the host/buyer's rules. However, it is important for the negotiators to face each other as equals so, within the rules, the visitor/seller is quite at liberty to suggest ways of dealing with the day's business creatively.

The creative agenda: Step 1

Enquire about your opponent's perceptions and priorities.

'I hope that we're going to be able to satisfy all your needs in this negotiation. To help us do that, it would be very useful to understand

what this project really means to you, and something about your priorities.'

You are entering an important stage – a kind of pre-negotiation. Keep your calculator in your pocket for the time being; the information and ideas you exchange with your opponent should be qualitative, not quantitative.

If your opponent is one of those who sees negotiation as a game of poker, he might want to keep his cards close to his chest – believing that every piece of information he gives out will tend to weaken his playing position. After all, if a poker player were to tell you his priorities at the beginning, it would be a simple statement: 'I want to deprive you of as much of your money as possible, whilst giving absolutely nothing in return.'

In such cases, you should lead by example. Try telling him something about your general priorities: 'I'm looking for an estate car without too many miles on the clock; my cash budget is limited, and if I can't find something I like within my price range, I will consider taking out some sort of finance package' or 'We are already established in this market, as you know, and now we are looking for ways to widen our network of distributors, especially as we are about to launch a new range of products – which are aimed at exactly the sort of people who buy their DIY products from you.'

Giving information like that does not weaken you, and it almost forces your opponent to respond in kind – giving you the kind of 'soft' data that will permit you to build a worthwhile agenda for discussion.

The creative agenda: Step 2

Make Sketchmap 2 together with your opponent.

'Why don't we talk through the agenda in general terms, to get a first idea of how the package might fit together?'

This is where you can bring Sketchmap 1 (>> *Planning*, page 86) out of your briefcase. Ask your opponent how it differs from his view of the situation. He will start to modify your sketch-map – or even to draw a completely fresh one.

Remember: big rings show important things, small ones matter less and overlaps show linkages.

Of course, this is a great time to get in a huddle around the flipchart.

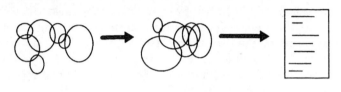

| YOUR PRIORITIES AND LINKAGES | → | YOUR OPPONENT'S PRIORITIES AND LINKAGES | → | THE CREATIVE AGENDA |

It is vital at this stage to be asking *open* questions – invitations to your opponent to tell you lots of things you never knew before. Remember that this is an early stage, and he's probably a bit guarded, so if you ask him yes/no questions, he will probably take refuge in one-word answers.

DEAD-END QUESTIONS

'So payment terms are important to you, are they?' 'Yes.'

'I see. And you have some flexibility on the batch size, after all …' 'That's right.'

'Could the insurance and transport questions be linked?' 'They might.'

'And you'd like to add a sale-or-return option to the agenda.' 'That is what I said.'

Avoid this misery by asking 'What? Where? When?', or better, 'How?', and best of all 'Why? … Could you elaborate?'

The creative agenda: Step 3

Dig beneath the surface.

'So you see payment terms as a crucial issue . . . why?'

'We didn't realise you had room for manoeuvre on the batch size . . . do you have a clear idea of what you'd like ideally?'

'It's interesting that you hadn't expected to discuss the insurance issue. If we include it, how will it influence your attitude to transport costs?'

'The sale-or-return option is an interesting new idea. What problems would that solve for you?'

Of course, none of this is any use at all if you don't listen to the answers (>> *Talking and listening,* page 151). At this stage you are sucking in information about your opponent's perceptions and priorities, so you can augment and modify the thinking you did at the planning stage; with a better understanding of what he wants and why he wants it, you can work out ways of letting him have it, while getting as much as possible of what you want. Note that all the examples above are qualitative questions; the quantitative bargaining questions come later.

In *Planning* we offer an analogy of the orienteer, before the event, studying a map of the terrain where the competition is going to be held. At this early stage of handling the process you are like the orienteer when he arrives with his team on site – learning about the state of the ground and the day's weather – and, more important, you are finding out where the checkpoints have been placed.

The creative agenda: Step 4

Get a complete picture.

'Is that your entire shopping list?'

Many negotiations turn sour when one party tries to introduce new variables, new criteria and new demands at a late stage of the process. Even if it comes about through absent-mindedness, it can seem like foul play (>> *Truth*, page 60).

Once again, the emphasis is on creating an atmosphere of openness and clarity, and taking into your next planning session all the information you need to redesign your package of proposals.

The creative agenda: Step 5

Get some forward momentum.

'All we have to do now is decide a running order for the agenda. Shall we start with something pleasant and easy?'

The agenda is not a series of independent points; there are many linkages and overlaps between them. You are planning a route through checkpoints in a forest, not climbing a ladder – so there might not be one obvious and logical pathway.

If you have, say, six items on your agenda, and you know that three will be tough to settle, while the rest will be nice and easy, you can do a bit of atmosphere-engineering in advance.

HOW TO RUIN EVERYBODY'S LUNCH, AND PART ENEMIES AT TEATIME

Tough > nice > tough > lunch > nice > nice > tough > goodbye

THIS MIGHT BE EASIER ON THE NERVES

Nice > tough > nice > lunch > tough > tough > nice > ciao!

Of course, other considerations will govern the running order of the agenda: it would be odd to discuss legal terms and conditions before you've agreed the general scope of the negotiation. But all other things being equal, it is a good idea to start on a high note, and so generate a positive momentum, and finish on a high note, so you can part friends.

The creative agenda: Step 6

Check for pitfalls and time bombs.

'Should we make sure our protocols are clear before we start?'

At more formal negotiations, and especially when you are on strange territory, you should clear certain questions up before it's too late:

- ❏ Who's taking the minutes?
- ❏ Which version – and perhaps which language – is the 'official' one?
- ❏ Which country's law of contract will apply?
- ❏ Is there anything else I should know about the local ground rules?

The creative agenda: Step 7

Take a time-out.

'We'd like to take a little time now to digest what we've learned, and perhaps modify our proposal.'

Your negotiation might at this point go through a reiterative loop, back to the preparation phase (>> *Timetabling*, page 111). This is your first major time-out, and it is very important. This is where you re-shape the ideas you developed during the initial planning stage – lowering your sights in some areas, perhaps, but aiming higher in others.

Ideally, the initial negotiation – designing the agenda – should take place in an afternoon session, with the substantive negotiation beginning the next morning. This gives you plenty of time to reconsider your proposal, and consult with colleagues at the hotel, back at head office, or by phone and fax.

WHAT THIS MEANS TO YOU

Invite your opponent to share his priorities with you, and give him an insight into yours.

Combine the two into a flexible, creative agenda, within the legal framework.

Take a break to think through what you have learned, and modify your strategy.

Remember this is a package deal. Nothing is agreed until everything is agreed.

When you return from your time-out with your new agenda and proposal, you must hope your opponent sees it the same way.

If he is inexperienced in negotiation he might try to nail you down to a final agreement on Item 1 before you move on to Item 2.

He might do the same, even if he has great experience. If so, he is trying to put you under pressure – and handling the process is all about avoiding such pressure.

In either case, it's time to be firm and direct the flow of the discussion.

Moving through the agenda: 1

Take a first canter round the course.

'Let's. work through the whole agenda, making *provisional* agreements where we can, and then see what the package looks like.'

Then you can get stuck in to Item 1, proposing, counter-proposing and bargaining, confident in the knowledge that it's all still hypothetical: nobody need be afraid of moving a little, since they are making no concrete commitment until the very end.

Each item on the agenda can be dealt with according to a tight–loose plan.

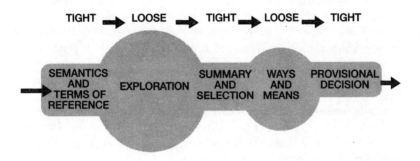

Semantics and terms of reference: Make sure that you're talking about the same thing and within the same limits. If your opponent speaks of 'a normal container-load of the industrial grade for me to package up in the usual way and sell on in my own market', there is plenty of room for misunderstanding. What are 'normal' and 'usual'?; is the industrial grade the same as your formulation?; are you sure 'my own market' means the same to both of you?

Conversely, you have a very clear idea of what you mean when you talk about '30 days' credit', but does he? Is that 30 days from invoice? From delivery? From the first day of the next calendar month? Or from the first working day? Or does it mean the supplier has to start shouting for his money after 31 days?

Exploration: This is the creative stage (> > *Creative bargaining*, page 63). You should by now have a fair idea of your opponent's position and why he has adopted it. He should understand your needs too. How many different ways might there be to satisfy your interests? This is time for 'What if . . .?', and 'Maybe we could . . .' and 'It's just a thought, but how about . . .?'

The language you employ at this stage should have a hypothetical, unthreatening flavour: no commitment on either side; let's just brainstorm.

If you are in a larger group, do everything you can to control the garrulous and encourage the shy: it might easily be the shy ones who have the best ideas for a creative agreement.

Summary and selection: The time comes to tighten up again. Give a clear summary of the position you have reached, and check any numbers and dates you have noted down.

Set out a short list of options as they have emerged. Explain why certain tentative ideas are now being excluded: 'That idea you had for manufacturing the shoes in Taiwan was attractive, but I think we'd better wait until we get above 20,000 pairs a year.'

Ways and means: This is where you shift from the hypothetical 'How would it affect you if we did $x/y/z$?' to more concrete planning: 'If you cover the costs of x, then we could take care of y and perhaps share the burden of z.'

Provisional decision: If all goes well, a preferred option should have emerged by now; time for:

Moving through the agenda: 2

Emphasise and celebrate positive achievements.

When people get *serious* about negotiating, they often forget about the Power of Positive Thinking – they leave out all the warm, happy signals that mean so much. You have invested a lot of time and effort in preparing for this encounter, and when your labours bear fruit, you should let your opponent know that you like the taste. Say:

'We've got very close to an agreement on this issue, but it's linked to several other items on our agenda, so let's set it aside for the moment and move on to our next point . . . This is very good, you know. We've hardly started and already we can see the beginnings of an agreement.'

Of course, there is no guarantee of such a happy outcome the first time you discuss a given item. You might reach deadlock at the ways and means stage. In that case,

Moving through the agenda: 3

Don't get bogged down.

'We seem to have got a bit stuck on this issue. Never mind: perhaps we can find a fresh angle on it later. Let's move on to the next item.'

Keep up the forward momentum. When you get to the end of the agenda, you will have some points still to resolve. This leads to the next process marker.

Moving through the agenda: 4

Short-list the remaining difficulties; take another time-out.

'We still seem to have a little work to do on items 2 and 5. Shall we adjourn now and see if we come back with fresh ideas?'

Then it's round the re-iterative loop again: time to re-package and look for fresh linkages and trade-offs.

What if there are more problem areas than there are areas of agreement? What if, in spite of all your efforts, the gaps are just too big to close?

This can be a crucial realisation: your boss is expecting you to come back with a deal, money and time have been invested, your opponent seems to have conceded as much as he ever will, and you are under pressure again.

It is time to look again at your esape route or fallback position – your best alternative to a negotiated agreement (BATNA) (> > *Planning,* page 88). The next round could be tough, and you must keep a sense of proportion – and recognise that a no-deal tomorrow will not be the end of the world. Otherwise, you might give too much away in the negotiation and end up with a bad deal – something worse than your BATNA.

The difficult gaps you still have to close are likely to be of two types: the arithmetical, where you can't agree a cost or price or deadline, and the personal, where you are failing to get on as people. In either case, you should be ready to take a step back and consider the difficulty from a calm distance. Not only that, but you should be ready to invite your opponent to do the same.

Moving through the agenda: 5

Redefine the basic arithmetic.

'Look, maybe we've been going at item 2 all wrong. Perhaps your needs could be served better by some sort of leasing agreement/a single bulk delivery/a team of your own people doing the installation, with supervision only from our side' (>> *Raising the game*, page 105).

Moving through the agenda: 6

Offer to change the process, to ease personal difficulties.

Personal pressure can come from your opponent at this stage – not because he's angry with you, and not as a deliberate bullying tactic, but because he's frustrated and nervous of failure. (Perhaps he hasn't worked on his BATNA.)

The pressure might come in the form of scowling, raised voices or strong language. Your opponent might begin suggesting that you yourself haven't been as diligent or as clever as you might: 'Have you *really* done your best on this? I thought you knew your way around this business.' And worse than that.

Don't respond in hot blood. Find time to think – by taking notes, asking to borrow a telephone, going to the toilet – or simply by saying 'I could use a quiet five minutes now.'

Look at this diagram. The frictions and heat are in the inner zone, where you and your opponent are trying to reach a result by negotiating; you should step outside to the cooler zone and think about the process you are involved in.

So when you go back into the meeting,

DON'T SAY	SAY RATHER
This delivery problem is totally insoluble.	You can see the difficulties we're having with deliveries.
It's going to wreck the whole project out there in the field.	All our hard work in this negotiation so far is at risk.
Bang goes my commission/ promotion/holiday in Honolulu.	It's a pity to waste it; some kind of agreement must still be possible.
And now I'm getting a headache and I want to go home. Please don't shout.	Let's go to a new place/field a fresh team/change the subject briefly.

The idea is to take a step back, or a step up, from discussing the substance, and instead discuss the discussion – focus on the negotiation rather than the outcome of the negotiation.

Instead of being at loggerheads over the price of transport, or who's responsible for changing the lightbulbs, you invite your opponent to look at the *process* calmly, and join you in your attempts to repair it. Cooperation rather than conflict.

And if you can't fix it between you, and you desperately want to find an agreement, you might decide to call in an outsider to help. If you choose a well-qualified arbitrator/mediator/ Solomon substitute, he will almost certainly use some of the techniques we have outlined in this chapter.

14

MOVEMENT

'There's always a gap between "us" and "them"'

There is always a gap to begin with. If there were no differences between you and your opponent, you could go out for a good lunch together rather than negotiating.

By the same token, if there is a difference, and neither of you is prepared to move in any way from your initial positions, you would be well advised to forget the idea of reaching agreement, and go out for lunch separately.

In *Creative bargaining*, we dwell on the dangers of the single-variable negotiation.

Translated into terms of *movement*, it means this: you and your opponent sit like ball bearings at opposite ends of a straight, narrow groove, and try to inch towards each other along it – using seduction or bullying to move the other guy, and offering reasons/pretexts/excuses for any moves you might yourself make.

If you start off too far apart, you might never get together – running out of dignified and realistic ways to close the gap.

If you sit tight and wait for your opponent to make move after move towards you along the groove, the time will come when he gets stuck and threatens to call the negotiation off. Then any move you make will seem clumsy, and the result of panic, rather than good intentions.

If you make all the concessions, crawling along the groove towards a static and triumphant opponent, then you are not negotiating as equals, and the relationship will suffer as a result.

A far more useful picture is presented by the balls on a snooker table – multiple variables, capable of endless inter-action, with plenty of space to move around in. The way you play will be different from classic snooker, which includes such strategies as forcing your opponent into making expensive mistakes; in this game you will be making suggestions to maximise your partner's score, and minimise his errors, while protecting your own target.

Closing the gap: Stage 1

Predict movement.

In *Handling the process*, page 117, we suggest that the discussion of the agenda – the deep agenda – form a first, quite distinct stage in the negotiation.

It is at this stage that you learn about your opponent's framework for the negotiation – perceptions, priorities, and potential for compromise: in other words, on which issues must he stand firm, and on which might he be prepared to move?

Naturally, the plans you then make for the negotiation proper will focus on the issues where movement is possible. No point in bashing your head against a brick wall.

Look at areas where he might be flexible, and match them up against possible movements on your part. That's where the trade-offs begin.

Closing the gap: Stage 2

Stimulate movement.

> If you would work any man, you must know either his nature and fashions, and so lead him; or his ends, and so persuade him; or his weaknesses and disadvantages and so awe him; or those that have an interest in him, and so govern him.
>
> Sir Francis Bacon (1561–1626), *Essay: Of Negotiating*

Bacon's was a cynical view. This quotation is popular among those who see negotiation as a manipulative process. It is interesting that Bacon was later imprisoned for taking bribes, and banished from parliament and the court, ending his days deep in debt.

Let us translate his observation into win:win terms:

> If you want to help somebody to a useful agreement, you must know either what makes him tick, so you design proposals to suit

him; or his needs and objectives, so you can show him how your offer matches; or his fears, so you can reassure him. Pulling strings with his boss is not within the rules of ethical negotiating, and will wreck your working relationship.

In *Talking and listening* and *People*, we deal with shaping your message to suit your opponent's personal perceptions. In *Creative bargaining* and *Raising the game*, we explain how to match appetites and goals.

Let us now consider how to deal with your opponent's fears. You have done what you can to offer a way forward, but he seems cussedly determined to stand his ground. When a person goes rigid in the face of common sense, it is always a good idea to ask: what is he afraid of? and then: how can I remove the fear?

Here are a few examples:

Fear of the Unknown

He has never before travelled the path you are suggesting. Give him a clear picture of the consequences: 'If we take x step, we will arrive in position y, and the consequences will be z. That's all; no further implications that I can see.'

Fear of Personal Regrets Later

He's attracted by your suggestion, but worried that he might look back on it and see a better option – too late. Reassure him that it's all hypothetical for the moment, and that you'll allow him to backpedal later: 'Of course you want to be sure you won't be sorry. I don't want to push you into an early agreement on this point. Can we just say that you're willing in principle, and move on to another item? Perhaps in the context of the whole package, it'll look even more attractive.'

Fear of Ceding Primacy

Naked ape stuff. If he moves, is he yielding? And if he yields, will you be the dominant male? And will you steal his food, territory and mates? Give him space to beat his chest a bit. 'You've clearly seen how useful this move might be to you and your side, and we'd be happy to let you have what you want. Tell us exactly how you see it working out for you.'

Fear Caused by Lack of Authority

He can see how the idea might work, but he hasn't been given an open mandate. Give him time to refer back to his boss: 'Perhaps you'd like to take a break at this point; certainly we would benefit from a ten-minute breather'. Or offer to talk to his boss yourself: 'Perhaps there's somebody you'd like to call in who could help us to clear this hurdle.'

Closing the gap: Stage 3

Make all movements conditional upon other movements.

To emphasise the two-way ebb and flow of concessions, discipline yourself always to say 'If you will . . ., then I can . . .'.

If you will guarantee £50,000-worth of bookings in the low season, *then* we can offer all your holidaymakers a free hire car for the week.

If you will persuade your finance people to release a 30 per cent cash deposit up front, *then* I can agree to a 90-day draft for the balance.

If you eat up all your spinach, *then* I'll see if there's some ice cream in the freezer.

Closing the gap: Stage 4

Respond to their signals by offering a movement.

Don't be afraid to move yourself; this is a two-way thing.

They might not be as direct as you; their signals might be more subtle. Be alert:

'As things stand, we can't lower our price' means 'We have room to manoeuvre on price, but we want you to offer an extra piece of business first.'

'I can't really see how I can take this package back to my members' means 'I think it's fair, but I want you to make a cosmetic concession to save my face.'

'I've never paid this much for a weekend in Paris' means 'There's a first time for everything; offer me one extra inducement and you've got a deal.'

WHAT THIS MEANS TO YOU

If your opponent signals, make a move. If he doesn't, give him a signal to move.

Closing the gap: Stage 5

Protect your main margin.

One advantage in treating the package as a whole is this: you can concede in all the peripheral areas, but protect the profit margin on the core business.

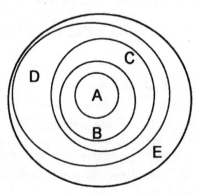

A = what it will cost you to build the installation
B = the profit you want to bank

C = your quotation for spare parts stock (cost plus a bit of fuzzy profit)

D = your quotation for training maintenance staff (ditto)

E = your quotation for user documentation (ditto)

As the negotiation advances, you can allow your opponent to 'squeeze' you on C, D and E, getting a better and better deal for himself and his company. Say:

> Maybe if you only held Class 1 and 2 spares on site, and we held Class 3 available for air freight, then we could drop the price . . . and if your staff were prepared to stay in a suburban hotel, we could bus them to our training centre every morning – fresh air for them, lower hotel bills for us, and a better price for you . . . and perhaps you don't need an expensive formatting on the operating manuals . . .

At the end of the negotiation, your opponent can point to a good day's work, and you have protected the all-important B – your core profit.

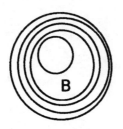

Closing the gap: Stage 6

Make your concessions carefully.

In Stages 3, 4 and 5, we have assumed that you will at some point make concessions. As you give ground, your opponent will be observing carefully, wondering 'how much further can I push this point?' Overleaf is an exercise in orderly withdrawal.

EXERCISE

During your negotiation, you are free to concede £1000. How to play it?

1: Say no for 59 mnutes and then yield the lot in one lump.

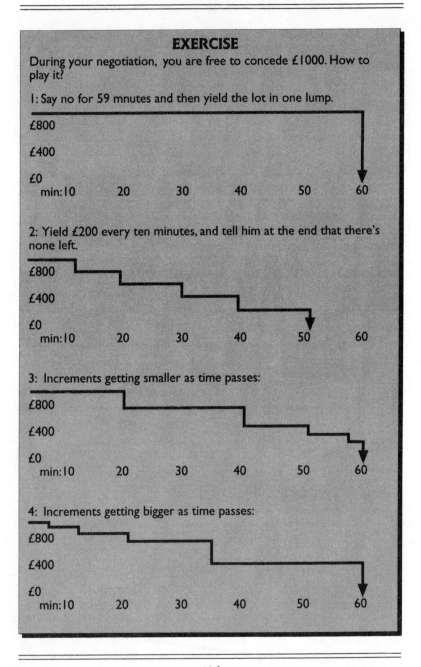

2: Yield £200 every ten minutes, and tell him at the end that there's none left.

3: Increments getting smaller as time passes:

4: Increments getting bigger as time passes:

The smart move is option 3. Your opponent will get the message that you are running out of concessions, and that he should be getting ready to shake hands.

Actually, the exercise is easier if you reverse it, placing yourself as the buyer – of a second-hand car, say. How should the seller come down from £5000 to £4600? Which strategy will give him the best chance of £4700, while still leaving you, the buyer, happy with the deal?

15

TALKING AND LISTENING

'I'm not a very good communicator'

Over the last 30 years, the work of managers has become increasingly specialised. As the work of the corporations became more complex, and as more and more information was produced, responsibilities were compartmentalised, and ideas flowed up and down the organisation through vertical pipes – but seldom between them. Simultaneously, the habit developed of talking to colleagues through their computer screens – the Internet, e-mail, Lotus Notes.

Not surprisingly, there is a whole generation of managers who (like you, if you have opened the book at this chapter first) feel weak in face-to-face meetings, especially when the pressure is on in a negotiation.

LEARNING THE TRICKS OF THE TRADE

Take heart: interpersonal communication is one of the most trainable skills. If you really want to do some work on your powers of talking and listening, the best thing is to go on a good course. Make sure:

❑ You are in a small group.
❑ The training methods involve lots of practice and personal feedback.
❑ There is space to discuss your own professional situation.
❑ The trainer has varied experience and is not a one-industry man.

Avoid courses which are described like this: 'The event is designed to provide delegates with the opportunity, within a structured learning environment, to explore the area of ABC and consequently enhance their performance in functions X, Y and Z'. It is a poor advertisement (see *Clarity* below).

If you can't go on a course, you can organise a training programme for yourself. Read this chapter, and

❑ Select one technique which would improve your own performance.

❑ Plan to use it in your next important encounter.
❑ Use it.
❑ Evaluate your performance and discuss it with a friend or colleague.

Then, when you have mastered the technique, choose another and build that into your repertoire in the same way.

The thinkers of ancient Greece and Rome have given us a complete analysis of rhetoric – the mechanisms by which we influence people when we talk – yet great communicators often seem to have some special power – charisma, star quality, 'a natural way with words', the gift of the gab. If we examine the performances of great talkers, we find that all the charm and magic is brought about by the judicious application of a handful of basic techniques, plus a dash of personal confidence.

Your confidence will inevitably grow as you master the same techniques, based on the ideas below.

THE TALKER'S TOOLBOX

In the context of a negotiation, you will do your most important talking when you are presenting your credentials and proposals, when you are standing up to pressure, and when you are helping your opponent to see things the right way – your way. The virtues you need on these occasions are:

Clarity: if they don't get your point, you won't get anywhere.
Assertiveness: if you're submissive, they won't take you seriously; if you're aggressive, they'll fight or flee.
Persuasion: if you can't sell your ideas, why should they buy them?

You can be clear without being assertive or persuasive, but you will never be persuasive without being clear and assertive.

We will deal with these three components in order: clarity; assertiveness; persuasion.

CLARITY

There is too much business jabberwocky – talk of 'facilitating outcomes' rather than 'getting things done'. It is a style of language that blurs issues, avoids responsibility and fails to lodge in the mind of the listener.

If you spend a lot of time reading company reports and technical documents that use a lot of ponderous words, you might tend to use the same style when you talk about business. If that is your habit, try at least to make your most important points in plain language.

Clarity tool 1

Use short, simple words and short, simple sentences in your key messages.

You will know from your planning stage what are the half-dozen main points you need to make in your first presentation – where you describe your credentials, and your hopes and expectations.

Prepare a mini-script for making each of these points – a couple of dozen direct, everyday words that your opponent can understand and remember.

DON'T SAY	SAY RATHER
One envisages a situation whereby provision of state-of-the-art multi-media maintenance data will be incumbent upon the supplier without additional premiums.	I take it there's a handbook on how to keep the equipment running? It would be useful to have it on CD-ROM. Can you throw it in free?

And to help him remember,

Clarity tool 2

Use visual hooks with your key messages.

Look at these doodles for a moment.

The visual part of your opponent's mind is his most powerful memory bank; help him to store your idea there.

Show graphs, diagrams and layouts. Tell relevant anecdotes about real people so he can create pictures in his mind. Use metaphors. Draw doodles as you talk (but don't annoy everyone by hogging the flipchart).

Each key message will contain a single idea. There are problems of clarity when you are juggling several ideas at the same time.

Clarity tool 3

Organise your ideas clearly, and show your opponent how they are organised.

In other words, your explanations and expositions should have a clear structure.

You would certainly have chapters, headings and paragraph breaks in a written proposal. When you are speaking your proposal they are even more important, as your listener can't flip back a page when he gets confused.

You can map your explanation like this:

We're discussing *fruit* (general topic), and we'll be focusing on apples, bananas and cherries (A, B and C). In connection with apples, I have three things to talk about (I – availability; II – quality; and III – price). Availability? There's a glut, as we all know (1). This means we can be very selective and offer you the best quality in terms of flavour (1), colour (2), and crunch (3). Like to try one? Now of course we are keeping our prices low: 15 pence a kilo at the dockside (1), with discounts for large orders (2) as per this price list. Now, turning to bananas . . .

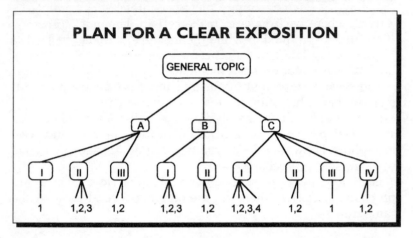

Ideally, your listener should be able to draw this diagram later from memory, filling in the subject headings correctly.

EXERCISE: VISUAL *versus* VERBAL MEMORY

At the top of the previous page (Clarity tool 2) there are 84 words and five doodles. How many of the words can you remember? How many of the doodles?

Clarity tool 4

Give a route map at the start, and regular signposts on the way.

Give an idea of the ground to be covered: 'We've got three main things to tell you, all to do with the guarantees we'll be expecting . . .'

Let them know when you're about to change direction: '. . . so that covers the general law on indemnity; I'll move on now to the way things are normally handled in our industry . . .'

Give warning of changes in the road surface – the mood of the meeting: '. . . which brings me to a rather sticky point, I'm afraid, where we'll have to make certain demands: compensation for lost production while the machine is under repair . . .'

One typical shift in mood comes when you stop describing things and start trying to make things happen – when you stop being simply informative, and start being assertive.

ASSERTIVENESS

To repeat: if you're submissive, they won't take seriously what you say. On the other hand, if you're aggressive, they'll either walk out or get aggressive back.

To be assertive is to stand up for your own rights, but in such a way that you don't violate your opponent's rights.

Some of your rights as an assertive negotiator are:

❏ To have needs that are different from your opponent's.
❏ To ask (*ask*) him to respond to those needs.
❏ To refuse his requests, with good reason, without feeling guilty.
❏ To negotiate as an equal.
❏ To stick to your bottom line.

Assertive behaviour

Show you know your rights by the way you act and the things you say.

Sit up straight, shoulders back, face the front. Don't fidget. Look him in the eye, don't mumble. Don't suck your thumb.

Choose a polite but firm 'register' – not brusque ('Explain that!') and not mealy-mouthed ('I wonder if you could possibly shed a little more light . . .'), but something in between: 'Could you tell us more about that?'

If your opponent begins to push too hard, don't escalate the situation. Point out to him that while it is important to you, this negotiation is not a matter of life and death: you are prepared to walk away and find other ways to satisfy your needs (>> *Planning*, page 88).

If you really feel you are failing in this area – by being either too submissive (putty in their hands?) or too aggressive (bull in a china shop?) – you should consider a training course in assertiveness – see the advice at the beginning of this section about communications training generally. An additional criterion: if you are a woman seeking help with assertiveness, try to get a woman to coach you. (If you are a man, you might not get the point of this advice, but women readers certainly will.)

PERSUASION

The next diagram shows a normal distribution curve. Suppose there is something you want to change, and you have to get other people's support. Always supposing your idea is a goodish one, a few of the people will grasp it and support it immediately (*the pro's*), a few will find reasons to block or sabotage your efforts (*the anti's*), and in the middle will be a big fence with most of the people sitting on it.

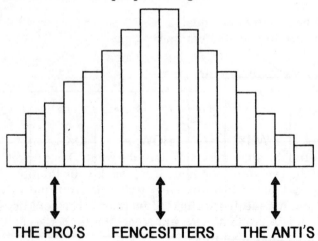

THE PRO'S   FENCESITTERS   THE ANTI'S

To get your bandwagon rolling, you give the pro's a clear description of your plan – see *Clarity* above. For those further along the axis, you need to build persuasive arguments.

The friendly, cheerful fencesitter who has the time to listen is the sort of person you hope to meet across the negotiating table. He wants to know how your argument is built.

Persuasion structure: 1 (reasons, means and caveats)

Make your main statement clearly ('This is the right idea . . .').
Support your main statement with reasons ('This is why it suits our needs').
Do the same with means ('This is how we can achieve it').
Anticipate your opponent's objections and show you are a realist ('OK, I see the drawbacks, but if we accept them, the benefits will be great').
Bring the reasons, means and caveats to life with supporting material.

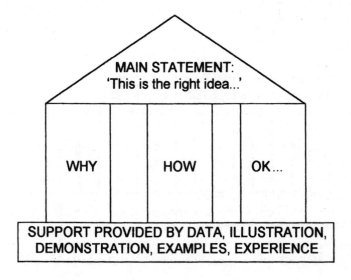

You don't have to make your points in this order, but when you finish, your negotiating opponent should be satisfied that you have dealt with all these aspects.

> Some of our storage tanks haven't been adapted yet to hold the new formulation, as you saw during your visit yesterday. So we will have a storage problem, at least for the first six months: here's the engineer's report (*reason* and *support*). We don't want to create unnecessary difficulties for your shipper; we've dealt with him before and we know he's a good bloke (*caveat* and *support*). Nonetheless smaller, more frequent deliveries would suit us better (*main statement*). What if we make a separate contract for the first six months' supply, and change over to bigger consignments when the tanks are ready (*means*)? We've done it before on contracts like this (*support* for the means).

For more sceptical fencesitters, or an anti who is prepared to listen, a punchier structure might help.

Persuasion structure: 2 (The four P's)

Describe the present Position, including everything relevant to your argument, and leaving out anything confusing.
Define the Problem to be overcome.
Set out various Possibilities for solving it, and evaluate them.
Adopt the best of these possibilities as your Proposal.

This time the running order is important. If you shuffle the stages around it gets very confusing.

Deliver each stage with confidence, and pause at the end. You should see a nod of agreement.

Position: You accept my description of the situation? (Yes . . .)
Problem: And my definition of the issue facing us? (Yes . . .)
Possibilities: You see, we've explored every avenue. (Yes . . .)
Proposal: And this is clearly the best solution. (Yes . . .)

A CLEAR ARGUMENT

It's clear you are looking for large volumes of apples, and expect to pay a low price, given the current glut. Is that right?

The question is where to get the best package of price, quality and delivery. Or is there something I've missed?

Now of course you could spend days shopping around to try and get a penny off here or there, but dealing with fly-by-nights isn't really your style ... or you could ... or alternatively ... I see you've thought all this through already ...

So we've put together a package for you that combines the best of all these options ...

Persuasion structure: 3 (feature, benefit, and you-appeal)

Select a key feature of your proposal or argument, work out what benefit this might bring to your negotiating opponent, and add a dash of you-appeal.

This is a basic sales technique. The salesman or advertiser frequently reverses the running order.

As a lover of luxury (*you-appeal*), you insist on the smoothest chocolate (*benefit*) – chocolate like this. It's made with 25 per cent real Cornish cream (*feature*).

That might seem excessive across the negotiating table, but consider this:

You can clearly do without the headaches of warehousing (*you-appeal*). Some sort of just-in-time delivery system would keep your storage areas clear and your production running smoothly (*benefit*). We have our own fleet of trucks and vans, and our transport department is used to just-in-time arrangements (*feature*).

If you use Structure 1, 2 or 3, your case will be given a fair hearing by all but the most hardened anti's.

Persuasion structure 4: Ju-jitsu

Ask your opponent to build your argument for you.

Ju-jitsu, the martial art that enables you (a small guy?) to drop your opponent (a big guy?) on the mat, is based on a simple principle: using the other guy's weight and strength in your own favour.

Suppose you have started with a simple polite suggestion – 'Do you mind if I open the window?', and he has refused permission. Your next step might be an appeal to reason: 'It's getting rather stuffy in here', or an attempt to sell the idea: 'If we freshen the room up a bit, we might get this business settled in time for lunch.' In some circumstances, an appeal at the personal level might work better: 'I'm beginning to get a headache, George. Any chance of a bit of fresh air?'

If all these fail, there are two obvious alternatives: you give up and suffocate, or you open the window without George's say-so and brace yourself for a rapid cooling of the atmosphere.

The ju-jitsu black belt finds a third alternative: 'What might I say, George, that would get that window open?'

In late 1995, there was a standoff in the all-party talks over Northern Ireland: the British Government refused to enter negotiations proper until the IRA had started to de-commission its weapons, and the IRA was refusing to comply – while stating that the blockage was all the fault of the Brits. The behaviour of heavyweight boxers was threatening to wreck the peace process. There seemed little hope at this stage for a ju-jitsu move from the British: 'What might we say that would get you handing in your Armalites and Semtex?' The American mediator worked the other way round: 'Tell me, Mr Major: what might the IRA say that would get you to the table with them?' The British offered this: a statement by the IRA that they intended to give up their weapons would be enough. (This concession produced a forward movement that upset the hard-liners within the IRA, and they started bombing again, and so the negotiation went into another re-iterative loop. In the context of 25 years of violence, the small incremental advance towards peace must be seen as a success.)

(For further ideas on how to counter downright hostility >> *Emotion, page 19).*

THE LISTENER'S RULEBOOK

There is a Swedish proverb: 'Talking is silver; listening is gold'. If you listen well during your negotiation, you will learn all the vital things you need to know in order to close the deal. If you also *look* as though you are listening well, you make a good personal impression on your opponent, and encourage him to loosen up.

Listening rule 1

Ask sincere, open questions so that you've got something interesting to listen to.

Closed questions – 'Do you . . .?. . . Have they?' might just get a yes or a no. 'Who? and 'Where?' might just get 'George Truscott in Basingstoke'.

The best questions are 'How?', 'Why?' and 'Could you tell me all about it?' (>> *Handling the process,* page 118).

Listening rules 2, 3, 4 and 5

Keep quiet and look at me when I'm talking to you.
Nod your understanding from time to time.
Take notes – it relieves the strain of eye contact and gives you thinking space.
Make encouraging noises: 'I see . . . quite . . . hmm . . .'

(The bedside manner of a good doctor combines all these elements.)

Listening rule 6

Use a playback loop.

Don't rely on your own listening ability; when your opponent is making important points, play them back to him to make sure you've got it straight.

'Do you mind if I go over that once again? ... try to summarise that? ... check my notes on that point? ...'

Obviously this is even more important when one of the negotiators is working in a foreign language, or when a Chinese and a Greek are negotiating in English as a lingua franca.

WHAT THIS MEANS TO YOU

If you want to build a lasting reputation as a good communicator, you should do as much work on your *listening* skills as on your *speaking* techniques.

If great talkers are credited with charisma, good listeners are often said to show personal empathy.

All other things being equal, who would you choose to represent you in a negotiation: a 23-year-old or a 46-year-old? Psychologists and many writers know what sort of attitudes and behaviour to expect from various age groups. The self-centred teenager is a bad communicator. The soldier in his twenties is described by Shakespeare: 'seeking the bubble reputation even in the cannon's mouth' – a death-or-glory attitude to be deplored in a negotiator.

Maturity in a negotiator comes when he has grown to understand that he himself is not very important in the scheme of things. He learns to hold on hard to his purpose, while letting go of his selfish perceptions, and considering the situation from his opponent's point of view.

That is the essence of good communication.

16

LANGUAGE

'I can't always find the right words'

A lot of people have doubts about themselves as communicators, and some think that not having a big vocabulary is their chief drawback. This is seldom so.

Good communicators who use high-flown, recherché words (otherwise known as 'orotund lexemes') usually do so for a bit of extra decoration and fun. If they overdo it, they cease to be good communicators.

They know that getting the message across depends on using simple, everyday words that people really understand. 'The right words' are the simple words.

NATIVE SPEAKERS

If you are an English speaker negotiating with an English speaker, or a Spanish speaker dealing with a Spanish speaker, and yet you have difficulty making yourself clear, then our best advice is in *Talking and listening: Clarity* (page 142), where we offer ways of constructing your arguments and putting them across cogently in everyday words and short sentences. *Keep it short and simple!*

If you can express things clearly enough, but want to add more power, subtlety or artistry to your messages, a training course will help. See *Talking and listening: Learning the tricks of the trade* (page 140). Otherwise, give yourself an occasional break from management books and business pages, and read some light novels, short stories or poems: widen your range of expression.

Language hints 1-3

Choose simple words for key ideas.
Use a few fancy words for decoration and fun.
Read outside your subject to develop your range of expression.

NATIVES SPEAKING TO NON-NATIVES

As a result of a series of historical accidents, English is the language of international business. If you were brought up speaking English, you would seem to have an advantage over the 'foreigners'.

But beware. The Hungarian or Brazilian across the negotiating table speaks good enough English for business puposes, but he could easily get confused if you speak to him as you would an Australian or even a Swede. And if he gets confused, he'll begin to feel anxious, and the atmosphere will deteriorate.

Language hint 4

When dealing with foreigners, grade your language sensitively.

If your non-native opponent speaks in short sentences full of up-to-the-minute business jargon, and limits himself to 'and', 'but' and 'therefore' as idea-connectors, you can assume he learned his English as a business tool, either by some commercial quick-learning method, or just by picking it up: 'We are interested to hear what you have to say about discounted cash flow forecasting and just-in-time delivery. Therefore I have asked my specialists to attend the next meeting.' You should adjust your level to match, and avoid long-winded stuff full of 'furthermore', 'notwithstanding' and 'consequently'.

If he uses rather formal vocabulary and ponderously correct grammar, it probably means he learned the language by traditional methods from a grey-bearded schoolteacher: 'We are somewhat perplexed at the means by which you have calculated an increase in price of three dollars the tonne . . .' In this case you should avoid too much executive-speak ('rolling over the incremental pay-offs into the next phase, to obviate punitive revenue measures . . .'), and also the idioms and colloquialisms for which English is notorious.

The happy medium is what is sometimes called 'offshore' or 'overseas' English. It is a rather colourless language, and draws

---

on 20th-century Americanisms when it wants impact ('Gut feeling'; 'ball-park estimate'; 'Just do it!'). But all over the world, hundreds of thousands of negotiators feel comfortable when they speak this language to each other. It is simple and unambiguous , and uses a simplified grammar and vocabulary. Technically, it is not a pidgin nor a creole, and it is not baby talk either. It is English as used by business professionals, but with all the lumps strained out of it.

Use simpler verb tenses, to avoid confusions like the difference between 'He did it' and 'He's done it'; very few idioms, especially avoiding things like 'We had a bit of a do', and 'Get on down!'; restricted vocabulary, so that 'carp', 'gripe', 'moan', 'lament', 'let off steam' can all be expressed by 'complain'.

If you are a native speaker, or virtually bilingual, and your opponent is less comfortable, then you should give him extra chances to catch your drift.

Language hint 5

Triangulate your idea.

Some of the things you say during the negotiation will be so crucial that you must be sure your opponent has grasped them.

Say these things several times in different ways, so your opponent can get hold of your idea by several handles, and reassure himself that he's got it right: 'We can only agree to these delivery charges if you repackage the goods according to our requirements . . . if you put the product in the cartons which we specify, then we will be happy to pay you more for transporting them . . . that's agreed then: new boxes, and we help you with the cost of shipping.'

(When speaking English to a foreigner, it is no good saying 'Do you understand?': the chances are that he will say 'Yes' just to be polite, and save you the trouble of repeating it all – even if he is completely lost. Ask him to tell you what he has

understood: 'just to make sure everything is clear, could you tell
me in your own words what this means?')

EXERCISE

Translate the following into overseas English. Our version overleaf.

1. You'd go a long way to better this offer.
2. I can see where you're coming from, but I still don't quite get it.
3. I'd fight shy of dropping the whole project, although we might have
   to consider cutting our coat according to our cloth.
4. We'll see you right on this one. Enough said?
5. I think we made a sound proposal, so now we'd like to sound you
   out on how it sounded to you.

OVERSEAS ENGLISH

(Answer to the exercise on page 157)

Of course there are thousands of possible versions, but here is ours:

1. This is a very good offer; better than our competitors.
2. I think I understand your general argument, but perhaps you could explain once more ...
3. We must ensure the project goes forward, but we might have to make economies.
4. We must promise to give you what you need. Do you accept that?
5. That's our proposal, and I think it's a good one. What do you think?

INDEX